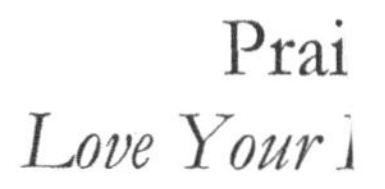

"*Love Your Family Again* is a great tool. I found myself nodding my head with some of the strategies, like 'yes, I'm on the right path. My small being is quite amazing.' Even so, as I continued reading, I'd raise my eyebrow in thought like 'Hmmm, that's another perspective or something I can try.' I really like the life situations that are …scenarios a parent has experienced or witnessed and the action steps that can be implemented immediately which give hope and relief that there are options. Dr. Marcie's patience and love for kids, as well as years of expertise, are definitely apparent. So glad to have this book as a reference."

—Danielle Scott, Mother of Juliánne Arruda
Speaker, Consultant, 5x Olympian

"As a coach of twenty years, I have read many books that direct people in actions when managing children. Most have a tidbit of information here and there. Dr. Marcie's book is a treasure trove of information for actually living in harmony with your family and experiencing joy on a regular basis. If you follow her direction, you *will* see results!"

—Kim Johnson, Mother of two
Coach

"This is a must-read for every mom, dad, and grandparent! Dr. Marcie's practical solutions with real-life examples reads like a parenting how-to guide. I love the exercises she has you try with your little beings. The tools and processes are simple but effective! I only wish I had this when my beings were little! But now as a grandmother of 2 beautiful children I get to redo!"

—Susie Carder, Mother of two, Grandmother
President, Motivating the Masses

"There are times, as a behavioral psychologist, when I have the need to consult with a child behavioral management expert and to refer patients for accelerated symptom relief. There is no better resource in my local professional network than Dr. Marcie! Now her strategies are available to anyone who reads this book, bringing the chance for success right at your fingertips. You will find her passion for bringing out the best in kids infectious and her interventions super-efficient, simple, and highly effective."

—Belinda Bellet, Ph.D.,
Mother of one, Clinical Psychologist,
Founder of Brooklyn Heights Behavioral Associates

"*Love Your Family Again* is brilliantly and beautifully created. I wish this book was around when I was raising my son as a single mother. Although my son is now an adult, this book allowed me to look at the way I communicate today and helped me realize that there are still plenty of things I could change to enhance many more relationships in my life. It's definitely a must-read for anyone looking at how they can show up differently for their kids and their family."

—Juliet Foster, Mother of one,
Owner, J. Foster Imagery

"In her book, *Love Your Family Again*, Dr. Marcie has created the handbook to conquer one of the greatest challenges parents encounter: fostering positive change in the behavior of children without creating an environment of heightened stress. *Love Your Family Again* teaches us to not only love the little people in our lives, but we can actually like them and start enjoying a happy and peaceful home again."

—Shyrlena L. Bogard, MD, Mother of two
Medical Director,
Advanced Center of Integrative Medicine

"Dr. Marcie is absolutely brilliant! *Love Your Family Again* is a roadmap of success for every parent. The guidance within this book has given my wife and I the support and direction we needed to eliminate the 'terrible' from our toddler's 'terrible two's.' This book is full of enormously practical advice and is an extraordinary guide to bring back harmony and joy to the family. We will keep this book as a handy reference for many years to come."

—Matthew S. Tadlock, Father of one,
Attorney

"This book is a godsend for parents dealing with the most challenging types of kids. Finally, a book with very clear, specific ways that parents can rein in their kids' worst behaviors while also figuring out how to give their children the support they need to minimize such problematic behaviors arising in the first place. Before I began working with Dr. Marcie, I searched high and low for a book like this, but it just did not exist. She is the best there is when it comes to kids who bedevil those around them and I have no doubt families will benefit immeasurably from this book."

—Elise Keppler, Mother of two

"My first thought when reading this book was 'Wow, where was this when my daughter was 5?!' When I first started reading, I thought it wouldn't be as relevant for me since my daughter is 16 now. Then of course I got to Scenarios 6 (He Acts Helpless), 17 (I'm in Over My Head!), 19 (My Children Are Ruined by Technology), and 24 (They Are *All So* Rude!). What I recognized is that there's something that can be gleaned from Dr. Marcie's well thought-out scenarios for EVERY parent, not just for those with younger kids. Her Scenario 'I'm in Over My Head' really resonated with me as it reminded me that we do need to cut ourselves some slack as parents, and remember to ask for, and get support when we need it. As a result, I will be recommending this not only to those with 'small beings', but also to those parents with older beings as well."

—Lori Granito, Mother of one
Motivational Speaker and TEDx Speaker Coach

Love Your Family Again

Love Your Family Again

The guidebook for becoming the parent of your dreams

Written By

Dr. Marcie Beigel

This book is sold with the understanding that neither the author nor the publisher is offering individualized advice designed for any specific family or person or to any individual's particular needs or other professional services. The information given in this book should not be treated as a substitute for professional advice. If expert assistance or counseling is needed, the services of a competent professional should be sought.

Statistics on the back cover are from:
http://onlinelibrary.wiley.com/doi/10.1111/jomf.12305/full

Published by Behavior + Beyond

LoC
Printed in the United States of America
For more information, visit: www.DrMarcie.com
ISBN: 0692942963
ISBN-13: 978-0692942963

This book is dedicated to you — an adult who is wise enough to ask for help to make the life of a child better. There is no greater gift than to teach a child that he or she is amazing and that learning is a life-long process. Thank you for being you.

TABLE OF CONTENTS

Introduction

Behavior is a big deal! Parents are not taught the basics, or much about how to parent at all. While there isn't a handbook or guiding force, there *are* countless books and courses to cover every area possible. It's confusing—the lack of information combined with an abundance of resources.

How can you raise kids who listen if you don't know how to make them listen? How can you raise kids without all the yelling if you don't have better tools?

My mission is to give you a working understanding of my behavioral secrets so that you can focus on doing what you do best—loving your family! You will enjoy your children so much more once you have the behavioral tools described in this book carefully stashed away in your tool belt.

This book is packed full of useful information and strategies to aid you in your home and outside your home. As a busy parent, you don't have the time or energy to read theory without direct application. Theory is only included here if it helps you understand the strategies I am suggesting. If it isn't useful, I did not include it. If you want theory, there are other books much better suited for that purpose.

Throughout the book, there are times when I will suggest that you take notes or record behavioral experiences. As such, I have left space at the end of each scenario, as well as at the end of the book, for your notes.

Another option is to purchase a notebook to use as your "small-steps journal." Find a specific place in your home to keep it. Document your experiences as necessary, and keep it in the same spot so you always know where it is.

Situation-specific versus concept-specific strategies

I wrote this book using concept-specific strategies rather than situation-specific strategies so that you will actually be able to apply the tools in multiple situations. Let me explain. When giving guidance about creating a fabulous behavior within a morning routine, each possible behavior challenge needs to be explored. Do your small beings not listen? Do they ask you countless questions? Do they simply ignore your directions? The list goes on and on. Therefore, each INTRODUCTION situation has several different concepts that may be layered together.

If you're looking for support in a specific situation, look at that situation and consider what the behavior challenge is that you are actually facing. It is not eating breakfast; it is *how* your small being refuses to eat. Since this book is written as situation specific, you can find the chapter about the refusal process to find your solution. It is the behavior concept that contains the answer you are looking for. So, I wrote a book full of answers for you! It's up to you to find the right concept for your situation.

There are a couple of ways to read *Love Your Family Again*:

Choice 1: Read the book through as a study of behavior, one section at a time. The scenarios within each section will help give you a full picture of how to apply the strategy of that section. Consider situations you currently face or moments from the past: What would you do/have done differently with them? Start challenging and changing your parenting philosophy to include behavioral tactics and concepts. Create an improved relationship with your children and watch your family thrive!

Choice 2: Read the Table of Contents page. Notice which scenario titles reflect a behavioral problem in your family. Read those scenarios and apply the behavioral strategies. Use this book as needed, like a cookbook. If you're selecting this strategy, you may consider reading the book with your child, depending on his or her age. It might surprise you how this can open the conversation about behavior for your family.

Both strategies are effective; the important element is to keep learning and keep coming back to the book! Behavior change takes time and is an ongoing process. The route you choose is personal and one you might make for a variety of reasons. Either way, use this book as a reference that you keep coming back to for behavioral guidance as you hit bumps in your family. Let it be a trusted guide—the handbook for which you've been waiting!

Three Keys to Unlocking Outstanding Behavior

Through my years working with behavior, I have noticed that if you wait until a problem explodes to address it, it will take longer to resolve. The best time to start addressing problem behavior is when everything is peaceful. This is counterintuitive, but critical. If you set a solid foundation by consistent and ongoing attention to behavior, you are more likely to get the behavior you desire in times of conflict.

Creating a solid foundation is easier than it sounds. There are three fundamental principles to unlock solutions for behavior problems:

1. **Speak with purpose, words matter.**
2. **Do more, actions count.**
3. **Choose honey, perspective is powerful.**

Each section of the book focuses on behaviors that are best solved with a particular principle. As you move through the scenarios, you will start noticing the behavioral patterns and the particular solutions grounded in each principle. Making these connections will help you identify the necessary strategies when challenging behavior arises.

All behaviors can change. Let me say that again because it is so important: *all behaviors can change.* You simply need to know the right way to make it happen and then put that knowledge into action. This book is designed to give you the knowledge you need to tackle the behavioral challenges in your family, one at a time.

Reality versus Privacy

Concepts and theory can only take you so far, so I have included stories within each chapter to help you more easily connect behavioral concepts to your family's situations. The stories about my life are true. They are mine to share, and I am happy to share them with you. The stories about children are not true in the literal sense.

The names and personal details are changed, and I combined several similar behavioral scenarios into one story. What is true in the stories about children or my sessions are the mechanics of behavioral strategy that worked for that child and with countless small beings. The privacy of children with whom I work and their families is of utmost importance. I would never breach their trust, even for your learning.

All of the concepts, strategies, and techniques described in this book are real. I have personal experience with all of them. I would never suggest a technique that I have not personally used successfully in multiple situations. Given the right situation and the right application, this book can and will change your life.

Love Your Family Again cannot replace individualized supervision, counseling, and personalized support. The strategies are general and the concepts broad. Each child is unique, and each behavioral situation needs to be individually assessed. Use this book as a guide, but always use your own knowledge and that of other professionals who know your personal situation.

The Term "Small Beings"

In these pages you will see a variety of terms used for humans who are under the age of ten years. If you are familiar with my writing from my blogs and articles over the years, you will know that I am partial to the term "small beings." There is a level of compassion and understanding we provide to other adult humans that is sadly not always applied to children. I use the term "small beings" to remind us that we are all human and deserve respect. Behavior has the same set of rules for beings of all sizes. Referring to children as small beings gives them back the humanity that is so critical for your family to thrive!

Gratitude

Thank you to all my teachers—there are too many to list here, but all of them influenced the knowledge I share within. Thank you to all my students—you are my greatest teachers. Thank you to beings big and small whose behavior has helped mine in big and small ways. Thank you to everyone who ever asked that I write a book—it has encouraged me to write and keep sharing. Thank you to my team (for this book, for Behavior + Beyond, and for my life)—I could not have done this without you all.

Happy reading!

Speak With Purpose, Words Matter

PART ONE

Once small or medium beings learn that you speak with purpose, their behavior changes. Your language, the specific words you use, is a significant part of your behavior. It is important that the words you speak match your meaning.

I am sure most of us believe we are honest, and I'm sure you believe that you are an honest person, too. On large, obviously important topics, you strive to be truthful, but what about the little things? Sometimes we say half-truths without even realizing it. You might tell your small being, "I'll be back in a minute," when you mean ten minutes. You don't do this maliciously, but small beings take note that you are not following through on your word. Yes, even before they can officially tell time, they recognize that what you said and what you did are not the same, and behavior is impacted.

Little ones cannot distinguish the significance level of situations the way adults do. When you tell your small being that he must come to the table for dinner but no consequence occurs when he doesn't come over, he learns that even though you said "must," that's not the case. Later on, when you tell him that he must go to the bathroom, he may not listen because last time you gave a direction using the same language, it wasn't necessary to follow it. Why should he comply now?

Only tell children they must do something if they truly must do it. Otherwise, use questions, give options, or make suggestions. Reserve directives for when you are ready to enforce their compliance.

Build a relationship with your children that is based on trust of your word. This also increases your credibility in their eyes. When your language and your meaning do not match, your children subconsciously shift their faith in you. They begin to model your actions (covered in more detail in Part 2) and test you more readily with behavior that is less than desirable. When your language and your meaning do match, your child easily trusts you and follows your directions. Day-to-day tasks become a breeze, and you have days so smooth you think you're dreaming.

Focus on the objective and observable actions you want from your children. If you tell them what actions you want to see, then it's clear when they follow directions. It is also clear to them what action they need to take. When you use vague language—for instance, "Be patient" or "Pay attention"—it is debatable as to whether your children are actually doing what you asked. Whereas, if you say, "I'm coming after you if you don't put that book away" or "Look at the book," there is no confusion about meaning.

One common situation in homes when parents do not mean what they say and say what they mean is meal time. Below is an example of how this could occur if one does not stand by the exact meaning of one's words.

It is a Tuesday evening and you just called dinner time to your family. You have prepared a lovely meal of chicken and broccoli and potatoes. All things your children eat. Maybe not their favorite, like pizza, but certainly something they have consumed countless times. Your youngest, Adisa, refuses to come to the table. This happens almost every meal, so you are not surprised. Yet you feel your frustration level rising. Out of the corner of your eye, you see him playing with Legos in the next room. You consider saying something, maybe a reminder to stop playing and join you at the dinner table, but ultimately you decide to do nothing, thinking maybe this is the day he will actually come to dinner.

Unfortunately this is not the day. By the time your older child has finished half his chicken, Adisa is getting louder as he plays with his Legos and he is starting to get riled up. Your older child is used to this and continues to eat, but now the play is getting out of control and you need to put an end to it. You say, "Adisa, you *must* come to the table. It is where the entire family is right now." You turn back to the dinner table and continue the meal.

It is almost the end of dinner, and Adisa did not come to the table. You call out to him again. Using a combination of threats and promises, you try to convince him to come sit down. He still does not come, and it appears that he is ignoring you. Now you start to worry that your older son will leave the table if you don't stay with him, so you let it go, thinking at least one child will be well fed tonight. Feeling exasperated and frustrated, you continue dinner without Adisa. About thirty minutes after dinner ends, you know Adisa will get hungry, rummage through the kitchen, and grab some yogurt and a granola bar. You feel terrible about your abilities as a parent and know that when you divide your attention, everyone loses, but you don't know what else to do.

The behavior plays out exactly the same way every night, but the extent to which Adisa does not listen to you always surprises you. Rather than being surprised, start asking yourself, "What can I do differently to change this behavior?" The truth is, behavior is interactive, so there is always something you can adjust to create a change in behavior. With the right tools, the adjustment will take you down a path of small steps toward the behavior of your dreams.

When you *speak with purpose*, this unfolds quite differently. You call your family to the table for dinner. In the next breath, you walk over to Adisa, take his hand, and walk over to the dinner table together. As you start eating dinner, he is at the table with you. You notice him start to wiggle in his chair but focus on the fact that he is sitting at the table and eating with you and your older son.

You chat with both your children about their amazing days, asking what were their favorite three things of the day. Halfway through the meal, he gets out of his chair and leaves the kitchen entirely. He sat for twelve minutes, and that is a long time for him, so you are impressed with how long he sat for dinner! You maintain focus on your son who stayed at the table. The meal ends without interruption. You comment, "I love when our entire family is together during dinner time." You mean it, and it's true! You would be much happier if Adisa stayed throughout the entire meal, but you recognize that behavior change is a process, and you know you will get there. You finish the rest of dinnertime feeling accomplished that your elder son ate his entire meal beautifully. In the back of your mind, you know that you will work with Adisa on his listening skills during less chaotic times, like the walk home from school or Saturday mornings while playing games.

Action Steps for "Speak With Purpose: Words Matter"

1. Notice the words you use.
2. Observe, without judgment, the small moments when your words and your meaning are not in alignment.
3. In that moment, notice the behavior of your small beings. Are there behaviors you want to continue? Any behaviors you would like to change?
4. If there are behaviors you want to maintain, great! Keep up those actions. If there are behaviors you want to change, consider what behavior you would prefer. Decide on what you want your children to do in that moment, and write it down.
5. Next to the list of preferred behaviors, write why each behavior is important. What makes that reaction better than what you are currently experiencing? Find clarity as to why this behavioral shift is critical. This step will keep you striving to change your behavior in order to change the behavior of small beings in your family.
6. Take small steps toward speaking with purpose, as in practice one to five times of doing this intentionally each day.
7. Celebrate each time you follow through on your word. Notice the behavioral response from your small beings. Celebrate with them when they have the behavior you desire.
8. Keep taking small steps until you speak with purpose a majority of the time. It is an ongoing practice for all of us!

Now that you understand how this rule can be applied in general, let's explore some specific situations where *speaking with purpose* will transform your family.

Scenario 1:

He Has a Hitting Habit

Dr. Marcie's Journey

It was November and I was on the subway, coming home from a visit to a family I work with through my private practice. In my head, I was going over the different strategies we worked on together that night. I was sitting in one of the forward-facing seats that connects to the seat behind it, a standard in New York City subways. Normally I (or anyone else on the subway) wouldn't interact with the person behind me, but a four-year-old small being—let's call him Erik—and his mother made themselves known. The mother was loudly and repeatedly yelling at Erik, saying, "no," "stop talking," "sit down," and "stop hitting." Immediately, my parent-training hat went on, and the behavior strategies in my head switched gears to this particular situation; he was clearly acting out to get attention. I fought the urge to offer guidance.

Suddenly, little Erik grabbed my hood and pulled. I turned around and said, "No. That is my hood." Rather than turning back around, I kept talking to him. I asked him his favorite color and talked about my purple coat and his blue coat. Then I paused, thinking maybe it was time to stop talking with him. After all, I was just a stranger on the train. He hit me.

This was my fault! I started talking to him when he pulled on my coat, which signaled to him that bad behavior gets my attention. You could see the horror on his mother's face as she yelled at him to sit down and stop. The challenge was, if I stopped talking to him then, something else undesired would happen again. Erik was not going to stop seeking attention. I got curious about what other ways he knew to get attention other than hitting. My guess was not very many, yet.

There were seven more stops on the train before I needed to get off. I quickly decided on the most effective behavioral tool possible to use in this short amount of time. I was going to teach him about what kind of behavior gets attention.

What This Means for Your Family

Hitting is never excusable and must be addressed, regardless of the person's age. In this chapter I will give you strategies to address hitting. In my private practice, I work with many kids with violent behavior, and change is always possible with substantial support, but this is not a guide for combating *consistent*, *violent* behavior in children. If you are not sure if a small being's conduct veers into violent territory, please reach out to me or another qualified professional.

There are lots of different reasons why small beings hit; it is a function of behavior. The form of behavior is what it looks like—the specific action that is taken. Most adults focus on the *form* of challenging behavior. However, to change behavior, you must focus on the *function*, which is why the behavior happens and what the child is trying to communicate. Behavior is a type of communication, and when you uncover what is being expressed with each hit, you can eliminate hitting. The function holds the information about how to change the behavior. You can learn more about functions of behavior in Part 5 of this book.

For small beings under three years old, hitting may be understandable if it fits with the pattern of a developmental phase. This is not an excuse for such behavior, but it can help you craft your response. If someone is hurt, however, hoping your small being will grow out of the behavior is not an effective strategy. When repetitive hitting happens, you need a plan.

Chances are, regardless of his age, your small being knows that hitting is wrong. Outside of the moment he hits, he knows that hitting is not the solution to his need for attention. He can recite all the reasons it is bad, yet in the moment of action, he cannot apply the logic to his action, which come from a defensive instinct. Your small being doesn't know what else to do, so he uses his hands. If he knew a better way, he would have used it.

In this case, there is no reason to ask your child why he hit someone; focus on changing his behavior instead. In the moment when your small one hits, resist your urge to ask, "Why did you do that?" There are no good answers to that question.

Hitting is not a sign that evil has descended into your small being and all hope is lost. It is up to big beings to see hitting for what it is—behavior that can be changed!

Make a plan with swift and consistent consequences for each time your child hits. Consequences do not always mean punishment, but are simply what happens immediately following a behavior. It is important that you know what you will do the next time your small being hits. Then you will always know what to do when this behavior occurs. Always veer toward action and less conversation. This is how I framed my response to Erik. Through my actions, I showed him that hitting did not get him attention in the few minutes we had together.

Your Small Steps

First, determine why your child is hitting. The best way to determine the function of the behavior is to track the behavior over several instances. Notice what patterns you observe and match that to one of the four functions of behavior listed on the next page. Putting in the effort to track behavior is necessary for effective results and will free up more time in the future, as you will reduce the hitting behavior disrupting your family.

Tracking the behavior will help you determine why your small being is hitting, so you can choose the fastest and most effective solution. You can use an ABC chart to record what happens right before and right after your small being hits, or you can simply keep a list of incidents noting the situation and its consequences. Either way, make sure to record the date, time, and what was happening at the time of the incident. Writing this down is critical, as memories are never error-proof. Creating and reviewing a chart with objective information will help you uncover behavioral patterns.

I recommend recording at least five incidents of the specific behavior in order to see a clear pattern, although for some small beings, more may be required. When you review your tracking, you can decide if the intention behind the behavior is to gain attention, to escape a situation, or to create a positive physical feeling (meaning the pressure hitting creates in his hand feels nice). These are three of the four functions of behavior. The fourth function is when there is a medical causation.

Because I only had a few minutes to interact with Erik, I used quick mental tracking. I knew that this small being was desperate for attention and that he often got it through hitting. His hitting was an attention-seeking behavior.

A. Hitting for Attention

Identifying the Function

This small being gets attention in some form after he hits. As long as the attention comes, so will the behavior. Look for acknowledgment from teachers, parents, or other small beings who are around.

Here are some questions to ask:

- Does the small being on the receiving end of the behavior (the child who is hit) have a big reaction that is funny to the child exhibiting the negative behavior (the child who hit)?
- Do multiple adults come over and talk to your child about hitting? How severe are their reports (on a scale from 1 to 10)?

- Do your child's teachers have conversations over and over again about stopping the hitting? Do you?
- Do other children (siblings, friends, peers) notice each time your child hits and comment on it?

Often times, after a small being hits, there are many long conversations with adults. If that is happening and the hitting continues, the chats might be something your child likes. While you conceptualize these chats as a teaching practice, your child might enjoy having undivided attention. Children often do not differentiate between good and bad attention. If he wants attention, he will find a way to get it, even if it is negative.

Hitting may also occur after a small being has not received attention for a long period of time. "Long" is a relative term, as two minutes may be long for some children, while thirty minutes could be the threshold for others. Notice how much time it has been since an adult engaged with your child. If the tracking shows that individual attention has not occurred for what the child perceives as a long time before each hitting incident, that is a huge indicator that the child is seeking attention.

Addressing the Behavior

Create a special schedule for your small being so you're able to increase attention before hitting tends to happen and decrease attention after it happens. If hitting for attention happens every five minutes, provide attention every four minutes. If hitting for attention happens every thirty minutes, provide attention every twenty-eight minutes. Tracking is critical in determining the schedule.

If there is more than one adult around in general, determine which adult will be providing the scheduled attention each day or portion of the day.

I used this technique with Erik, the child on the subway. I observed that it took him thirty seconds without attention to act out. Turning to face him again, I asked if he wanted to sing the ABCs. Without waiting for an answer, I began to sing. When his hand came back up to hit me again, I met it, held it, and kept going. He was hitting because he wanted the attention to continue; it was the only thing he knew to do to keep me engaged. As I kept singing, he started to realize that he could get attention simply from looking at me. As long as he did not hit me or anyone else, I kept talking and singing with him. Small, simple steps go a very long way if repeated over and over again.

B. Hitting to Escape

Identifying the Function

Some children will hit to get out of something—in other words, to escape. If they do not have the language, skills, or capacity to get themselves out of a situation, hitting is an easy option. Hitting during cleanup often results in talking with a parent instead of cleaning up. Hitting during a birthday party often results in leaving the party, which may have been too loud and chaotic for the child. Hitting during an academic task often results in a change in activity and getting out of learning things that may have been too challenging or too easy. If your tracking shows that removing a small being from a situation is the consequence for hitting, then this is an escape-seeking behavior.

Addressing the Behavior

An effective plan to change this behavioral function is to not allow the child to escape after hitting and to find a way to give him a break *before* hitting occurs. Practically, that means giving your child breaks throughout the day, especially during challenging times. Challenging times do not have a universal definition; they are dependent on the particular child in question. Think about those times of day, activities, and circumstances that cause disruptive behavior from your small being. These are his challenging times.

Giving your child a break could include having him run an errand for you, asking him to get you an object from across the room, or sending him to the bathroom. These are all ways to give your child a break without directly offering one. If you have the room, create a space in your home for breaks, and initially send your small one there when needed. You will know the time frame from information you recorded during behavioral tracking. Gradually, teach your child to ask for breaks so the regulation of needing a break becomes internalized and appropriately communicated to the adult "in charge".

When a hit does occur, it's important to not let the action of hitting change the demands of the moment. Keep your child engaged in the challenging activity even after a hit occurs; stay focused on the topic and address the hit later. This will teach the small being that hitting does not result in getting away from an undesirable activity.

Just like with attention-seeking–hitting, have a clear plan in place. When a hit happens, you will be prepared and will be able to easily carry out an effective consequence.

C. Hitting for Self-Stimulation

Identifying the Function

Sometimes a small being will hit because the pressure of the hit or the feeling on his hand feels good to him. When the pattern you find from tracking tells you that hitting happens at random times and with random consequences, it may be that he likes the physical feeling that results from hitting. Notice if your child likes big hugs or other physical interactions that provide a similar feeling to what may be experienced during hitting. This is not a sign of something being terribly wrong with your child, but simply that he is seeking a particular feeling. All humans enjoy certain feelings; your child is no different.

Children will engage in actions they like to receive. If your small ones like to feel deep pressure, they may believe that hitting feels good to others, as it provides a deep sensation. Hitting is sometimes confusing for kids, as in some moments when it is a playful act, especially when everyone is laughing.

Addressing the Behavior

For a child who has a problem with hitting, you must make it clear that hitting is never fun, funny, or playful. Clarity is key here!

Teach your child a way to get the same sensory input through more appropriate actions. You can teach him that hitting a ball or playing various hand-clapping games are appropriate occasions where hitting is okay. Maybe tickling instead of hitting can get a similar physical connection and is something your child may do with consent.

The Smallest Step

Regardless of the function, at the very least, stop having so many conversations about hitting. The repeated dialogue will not get rid of the behavior. It just brings attention to the fact that your child made a bad choice, and no one feels good when there is a constant reminder of past mistakes.

NOTES

Scenario 2:

She Never Stays in Her Seat

Dr. Marcie's Journey

This is a behavior challenge that spans across home and school. Your child is constantly shifting, moving, and getting up, and it drives you crazy. First, she needs a drink of water. Then she must get her favorite stuffed animal, followed by a bathroom visit. The list of things she needs that require getting out of her seat is extensive. The reasons to keep her in her chair are few. You notice that during quiet play with her dolls, during which she can lie on the floor, she's able to stay put. The contradiction can be frustrating, but there is certainly a behavioral cause.

While I've worked with numerous kids with this difficulty, a true understanding of this behavior came from a learning experience of my own. I was in a nine-day workshop that required countless hours inside one conference room. While it was in a beautiful location (Fiji), most of my time was spent within one room with four walls, listening and learning.

The room was set up with 75 chairs in the front of the room and 75 red trampolines in the back of the room. On the second morning of the workshop, we began a daily ritual—jumping on the trampolines with some great music playing. It really got my body ready to learn and focus. The instructors told us that we could return to the trampolines at any time. Interesting!

I soon found that I was on a trampoline, either sitting with crossed legs or bouncing, for more than half of the workshop. It helped me listen better and stay focused. My attention was continually on the speaker while my body was in motion.

When I tried to sit in a chair, after about an hour, I became distracted. I started shifting in my seat. My leg fell asleep often, and my back felt stiff. I was so focused on my body that I was missing valuable information. On the trampoline, I could sit and listen for hours. Other people were jumping throughout the lectures as well. It made for a very energized and engaged audience.

After I returned from this conference, I visited a friend who is the director of a school for children with special needs. We walked through the school and talked about how her children were doing and what new techniques were being used in the school. They have a great sensory gym where kids can go when they need to move their bodies. It works well, but sometimes students are out of the classroom too much because they're in the gym. While we were walking, I kept picturing trampolines in different spots. I kept hushing that idea, as it would be crazy to make that suggestion. Luckily, I eventually spoke up. We'll discuss the results later in this section.

What This Means for Your Family

Does my experience at the conference remind you of any of your small being's behavior? Would it seem like she would be better jumping, standing, or sitting on a trampoline for dinner than in her chair? When we traditionally think about listening and learning, we think about students sitting at a desk and a teacher in the front of a classroom teaching. The desks are usually in rows that fill the entire classroom. At home, this vision does not translate, and it becomes confusing about how to get your small one to sit still for anything. Do you hear from your child's teacher that she has a hard time sitting still? And while you want to work on it at home, you have no idea how to teach this skill. Sitting is a foundational behavior and will it transform your home life when your small being can do it easily.

Does your child need to sit all the times you want her to sit? The most important thing is that she pays attention when you speak and stays engaged when doing a task. Is it a problem if she needs to do something different with her body to facilitate paying attention? Rather than accepting the idea that all children need to do something specific, let's question our thoughts first. Why is sitting still important? It's not a measure of attention or focus.

Is the objective to teach her how to sit or how to listen? All too often we get the two confused. Learning how to be seated in a chair at a desk or table is a valuable skill for her to have. However, it is not necessarily something she needs to do all day. Your child is most likely learning how to control her body as she is struggling to sit still throughout the day. Finding reasons to get out of her chair is not an act of defiance, even if it feels that way. It is a behavior, and she needs to be taught how to do it differently.

There is also an opportunity to teach your child about individualization here. You may be concerned that by making an exception in certain situations, she will start moving around or standing all the time. If you let her stand in specific situations, you do not need to allow it at others. Before she constantly asks about individual situations, bring it up to her. Talk about how different situations feel different and have different needs. For eating, she needs to sit because of the physical process, yet during art projects it is safe to stand. You can also talk in general about differences, which is a great conversation if you have more than one child. Children have different-colored hair and eyes. They also have different strengths. If one of your small beings asks you why her sibling is standing or if she says it's unfair, you can reference the individualization conversation you have already had. "Each of us has a unique set of needs, and at this moment Marcie needs to be standing." This will make for a quick and easy conversation because everyone will have a reference point for the explanation.

Your Small Steps

Assess if it Is a Problem

The answer to this behavioral challenge may be a simple switch in your expectations. The desire to have your child sit might be more about what you think a situation "should" look like and less about the reality of this particular activity.

Does she need to sit down? As long as she is paying attention and being respectful, the answer is no. Let her move her body. Support her physical needs. Find a location where she can stand or move that will not disrupt other family members, as each being in your family has a different set of needs.

It is possible for one child to be engaged while standing, lying down, or sitting on the floor. Consider what this particular body needs. Consult with a professional like an occupational therapist or physical therapist or behavior therapist, if needed. Prioritize you child's physical needs over your opinion of how an activity should look. Try a variety of locations and different methods to find a variation that allows her to be at her best. If your child is not paying attention when she moves, then she *does* need to sit in her chair.

You may find that there are moments when she doesn't need to sit in her chair. Get clear on when it is important, and communicate this directly.

Avoid repetitively telling your child to sit down and sit still. If you find that she is not listening to this direction, it is most likely because she does not know how to get her body aligned with your request. If you are going to tell her to sit down, make sure it is a requirement for the particular situation.

The more you repeat directions that your small being ignores, the less control of your children you ultimately have. Speak with purpose by only enforcing sitting rules when they are absolutely necessary.

Plan of Action

Decide when your small one must be seated and when your child may have alternative seating or movement possibilities. Make sure that your decision reflects realistic expectations for the age and abilities of your child. Adjust your rules as your small being learns the skill over time. For example, you may let her know that during breakfast or homework, she needs to be seated for the first five minutes. After that, she may move her body as needed. Once this expectation is set, you may gradually increase the time from five minutes to seven minutes to ten minutes to the entire meal.

Let your entire family know these guidelines. When you are transitioning to new moments in the home, communicate the sitting needs for that time, activity, or event.

Determine if there are any modifications that need to be made for your child, if she is having difficulty. Work out what support you can give when she is having a hard time sitting. Be proactive in offering support. Have a technique ready, like a cushion that your struggling small being can sit on for a short period of time.

Create a plan that will allow your child to be successful, and know what the consequence will be if sitting does not occur. Does her chair get moved closer to you? Do you move her to a different location? Do you warn her? Is she no longer allowed to participate in a fun activity? You may also ask your child to sit for the first few minutes of an activity during which she usually stands. This will allow you to remain calm when additional support is needed.

I also encourage you to think outside the box. While on the tour at my friend's school, I finally pointed to a corner of one classroom and said to her, "That would be the perfect place for a trampoline. This way kids could get a movement break and stay in the classroom."

A huge smile came over the director's face. That was the solution to their problem! Before I left that night, she had ordered a trampoline for every classroom!

The school developed some great rules around trampoline use to keep everyone safe and comfortable. Only one student may jump at a time and only when there is an adult in the room. The messages I got from my friend in the following weeks were incredible; students were having fun, dealing appropriately with their need to move, and spending more time actively learning in the classroom. Might be something to consider adding to your home!

The more proactive you can be to set clear and realistic expectations, the more your small beings will stay in their seats when you need them to do so.

The Smallest Step

Only give reminders to sit down when you have the capacity to follow through and ensure that your small being sits down. Empty directions will only teach your child she does not need to listen to you, which is a lesson you never want to impart.

NOTES

Scenario 3:

He Is the Family Chatterbox

Dr. Marcie's Journey

Your small being can talk without end. Sometimes he talks about things that are relevant, but just as often he chats about what is happening outside the window or in his imagination. His voice, no matter the daily events, is the constant sound track of your home. Every way you say it, "It's quiet time" or "No more conversations" or "Stop with all the words!" works for exactly three seconds, when you are lucky. At times, you've wondered if it is a disorder, but your pediatrician reassures you that it is not. You think you have tried everything, including ignoring him, punishing him with no dessert, sending him to his room, and using a reinforcement chart, but none of it has worked. The entire day you are distracted, and you are at your wit's end!

I was this child when I was a small being. In some moments it was a great asset, but at other moments it got me into trouble. My dad worked in Manhattan, and my family lived in New Jersey. He drove to the station every day and left his car in the parking lot before riding the train or bus into the city. Some nights my mom would pick him up, and we would go directly to dinner. Afterward, we went back to the station parking lot to pick up my father's car.

He was often very tired by this point in the evening, and it was here that my chatterbox skills came into play. My mom asked me to ride home with my dad and continuously speak to him so that he would not fall asleep. I took this job very seriously and would talk nonstop. And I do mean nonstop! It was important to me! We always made it home safely, and I felt that my communication skills were valuable.

I use a version of this technique with the small ones in my private practice. Vinnie was an eight-year-old boy with an ADHD diagnosis and a gift for gab who remembered the best stories from his day at the precise moment we sat down to do his homework. He wanted to share them because he was worried that he would forget. I didn't want to stultify his creative storytelling, but I knew he was chatting to escape his homework. I began to craft a plan of action that balanced the conflicting needs within this small being.

What This Means for Your Family

Let's be clear: talking in and of itself is certainly not a problem behavior. Take a moment to celebrate that your chatterbox has a lot to share!

Talking when he needs to listen to directions or play independently is the problem. It is important that you teach your small being when to talk, when to listen, when to play, and when to work.

Chances are your child is not capable of completely stopping his talking. What you can teach is when it is okay and when it is not okay to talk. Provide your children with clear guidelines so they know when they can indulge their communication skills.

Your Small Steps

Here is the good news: behavior is always changeable! The processes below will help you change undesired behavior.

Creating Expectations

You may use a chart like the one below to make clear appropriate talking and listening times. There is no better way to solve chatterbox syndrome!

Talking Is Great	Talking Needs to Wait
On our way to school	While I'm on the phone
While playing	When I'm talking with your sibling
During meals	After bedtime
During bath time	While I'm reading to you
In the car	During adult-only conversation

By all means, customize the elements of the chart to

what works best for your family and your small being's chatty patterns.

Creating a Schedule

I used a schedule for Vinnie, the eight-year-old with ADHD, in my private practice. I made sure that all adults who spent time with him were on board with the new program. There were three parts to homework time: quiet time, talking time, and storytelling time. Each day, the order of these segments shifted.

During quiet time, the small being needed to read or do worksheets quietly. Talking time included vocal quizzing for a test or engaging with an adult for homework help. Storytelling time was a requirement, even though it was not assigned by school. It was important that it was not something he only did when he wanted to share; we utilized his talents for a creative project. He and the adult in charge wrote down his stories or recorded them, slowly working up to a portfolio. Just like my talking job as a small being, he had a storytelling job. Knowing exactly when and why he had to tell his stories made it easier for him to be quiet when necessary.

There is no need to hate this behavior in your small being; you simply need to find the right time and place for it. A schedule can help you do this. While it is usually not possible to a have a schedule that meets every moment's needs, you can certainly increase compliance. Schedules give order. When you post a schedule in a visible spot, it lets small beings know what is coming and is a reference for them to check when they forget.

Look at your daily schedule (or consider creating one if you don't have one), and find times when it is okay for your child to talk with you. It could be as short as a three-minute break that you work into the daily chores or as long as a thirty-minute period, like dinner time. Indicate the talking times on the collective family schedule. Yes, you are going to talk at other times throughout your day, but this specific scheduled time will have a bigger impact than you expect.

Communicate in age-appropriate terms that there will be chatting time and non-chatting time. During non-chatting time, your children are only able to speak about things that are related to the topic at hand. This will also help with focus and attention of tasks. Take some time to practice the behavior with your small beings. Feel free to exaggerate the differences between acceptable and unacceptable chatter when you practice; this is the time for corrections. During regular daily activities and life, do not comment on the talking. Simply refer to the timetable.

It is very important that you stick to the schedule. What you say is critical, and your chatterbox will trust that the time to talk is coming. Once your child masters this behavior, you can gradually adjust the conversation times and make it more flexible. Make this a slow adjustment. If you move too fast, the effectiveness of your schedule will diminish or disappear. Be transparent about the shift in schedule with your small being.

The Smallest Step

Stop giving disruption attention. Continuously saying, "stop talking" will not work. It only adds to your frustration and teaches your small being that they don't need to listen to you, especially if they don't stop talking when you say, "stop talking."

NOTES

Scenario 4:

She Asks the Same Question Over and Over and Over Again

Dr. Marcie's Journey

I'm very flattered when parents and teachers divulge to me that when faced with a behavioral challenge, they sometimes ask themselves, "What would Dr. Marcie do?" It often happens that parents will ask each other this question when trying to determine how to respond to their small being. My favorite is when the family then tells me about it. :)

When I am in a family's home, sometimes I end up diving in and playing directly with the children. When I am with a family, I am there to teach and model. One of the small beings in this family asked repetitive questions, mostly due to her own anxiety and desire to control the conversation. One day I was reading a story with three sisters, and I asked the youngest, Lina, "What was your favorite part of the story?" She responded with her question of the day, instead of the answer to my question.

My response tactic was to speak with purpose, so I repeated my question, "What was your favorite part of the story?" She repeated her question, and I did so again with mine. It was a dance. Eventually, after about the ninth round, she answered me. The parents watched the entire interaction, shocked that her sisters just sat there watching as well. They had never seen someone stick to his or her own question for so long, and when faced with Lina, they wanted to see what would happen next.

A few days later, in a similar situation, her mom asked Lina to answer a question about breakfast. She answered with a question as she did in the previous anecdote. But, this time, the family came together to support the mom in an amazing way based on the behavior that was previously modeled for them.

What This Means for Your Family

A small being repeatedly asks a question for one of three reasons:

- She is comforted by the routine and structure of the same answer. The predictability feels good to her.
- She does not believe your answer because sometimes you shift your response. Also, throughout the day, you occasionally do not follow through on your word. Brush up on it and she will start to believe your answers.
- She wants attention. Social dynamics can be tricky and maybe your child has not mastered other ways to consistently get your attention. Asking the same question over and over is a surefire way to get you to speak with her every time!

Your Small Steps

Consider what you model. Do you ask small beings the same question over and over again? Sometimes parents do this unintentionally, so notice your own behavior. If you use this tactic purposefully, consider why you do this. If you want to keep it as you find a benefit, consider embedding a conversation about the appropriateness of this kind of repetition. Create a teaching moment to impart to your children when it is fitting to restate yourself. Asking repeated questions as a parent to keep your children on task, build creativity, and promote deep thinking can be valuable. Make sure to talk about this with your children outside of those moments when the repetitive behavior is happening.

Here are some other strategies to use to reduce repetitive questions, applicable for all three causes of the behavior:

- Let your small ones know that you will always answer questions. Some children are afraid to ask a question. Make sure you encourage those times when your child is curious and wants to learn more. Teaching that there is no dumb question is something I love so that children know they can feel comfortable to ask anything.
- Tell your small beings that you will answer all questions one time and will let them know if the answer changes. Make it a family rule. As an added bonus, you can teach your children to hold this rule true for all personal interactions, even outside your family.

- Stand firm with your decision to answer questions one time. The second time a question is asked, perhaps say, "What was the answer last time you asked?" in a flat, monotone voice. Make your small being accountable for listening to your answer the first time. Once your child gives you the answer, congratulate her for remembering and move on. Do not use punishing comments or exacerbated reminders.
- If she does not know the answer, then remind her that this will be your last time responding to the question. Give her the answer or motivate another family member to answer, if someone else is present. Immediately ask her to repeat the answer to ensure that it was heard and absorbed this time.
- If your child asks the same question a third time, say, "We already talked about this," or "I answered that already." Pick one phrase, and use it every single time your child asks you to repeat an answer. Do not answer it again.

Provide positive attention to your child when she asks a lot of different questions. Ask her to help you with activities or praise her when she asks a question one time. Notice the good things your small being is doing and point them out. The positive reinforcement provides the social interaction your child needs. It will also highlight how to get attention from you without asking the same question over and over.

Make sure you accurately answer questions. If you are not consistent with your words and answers, children will be justified in asking the same question over and over again. Examining your behavior and language is an important part of behavioral change.

Practice speaking with purpose. The more you can do this throughout your day, the more your children will listen to your words and not ask for confirmation. We all need some practice with this. The inconsistencies of our language have a big impact on behavior. Take small steps to be clear with your language, and you will see big improvements in behavior.

I used the above plan with Lina's parents. When the mom was alone with her daughters, she asked a question, and Lina repeated a question of her own. She paused and thought, "What would Dr. Marcie do?" before asking Lina the same breakfast question. After the fifth round, the mom started to get frustrated. This is to be expected, as she had never tried this technique before. The eldest daughter looked at her mom and said, "That is just what Dr. Marcie did Tuesday!" That one sentence gave the mom the conviction to keep going. It took her thirteen tries before Lina answered. The family watched, and when it was finished, the mom looked at her oldest daughter and said, "Yes, that is exactly why I was doing it. Dr. Marcie is really helping us all with our behavior."

The Smallest Step

Answer repetitively asked questions without expressing negative emotions. When you let your children know they are pushing your buttons, you unwittingly motivate your child to continue. Let's face it, small beings find it fun to frustrate big beings.

NOTES

Scenario 5:

He Is a Child Who Needs *All* My Attention

Dr. Marcie's Journey

No matter the event or the activity, your small being has questions and comments or does things that you simply cannot ignore. As hard as you try, you find that you end up talking to him all the time. While you think of yourself as a kind human, all you experience in the face of this behavior is frustration. In addition to earning my doctorate, I also obtained a craniosacral-therapy certification. In one of my first classes, during a break, I walked over to my teacher and said, "Can I ask you a question?" I will never forget his behavior when handling the question, which I now use as a model for how to deal with students' needs at inopportune times. He looked up at me, looked at the papers in front of him, and said, "I need to do two things before I can speak with you." I expected him to walk away from me to go take care of the two things and forget about my query. "Oh well, it happens," was my initial thought, but I was truly surprised with what he did next.

What This Means for Your Family

Time is precious. There are only so many hours in a day and only so many hours (sometimes minutes) you have with your family. The balancing act of getting everything done in the time frame you have is one of the magic tricks of being a parent. It is remarkable. Go ahead—pat yourself on the back for just a moment for all that you fit into each and every day.

Your attention will never be evenly spread across all commitments in your life; actually, it will never be balanced across your children. You will never spend equal time with each child, nor should you. Some children thrive with attention. Others behave best when working independently. Other small ones are shy and resist constant attention. Knowing the specifics of what each of your children needs is the gift of a great parent. It does require that you parent based on what your child needs, rather than how you want to parent.

Your Small Steps

Small beings all have different needs, and one child might genuinely need more support or attention than another. This reality can feel disproportionate, overwhelming, or, frankly, impossible to manage. The first step is to simply accept that one child requires more energy from you. How can you feel more productive when attempting to meet the child's needs? Take one small step at a time, and notice when there are any improvements in behavior.

Here are some strategies to allay the demands for attention:

1. Stop saying that you cannot talk to your child, but then proceed to talk to him. Many parents say "It's not time for questions" and then answer a child's question. The persistence of your child asking or talking to you should not change your answer. If you say it is not a good time to speak with you, then do not interact, no matter what behavior comes afterward. It is easier said than done, but it is absolutely critical to changing the behavior. Here is the trick: You don't need to say that it is not time to talk. If this child asks a question, you could simply answer him. It's all about speaking with purpose!
2. Give him attention! Face it, he will act up to such a degree that you can't ignore him, so give him tons of attention as soon as he asks for it. If you are able to spot the precursor to the problematic behavior, give him attention before he goes to that disruptive place. Create a timetable so you know when to give him attention. If you find he needs attention every five minutes, give it to him every four and a half minutes.
3. Get him invested in being your helper! Provide him with special tasks like getting you a book from the other room for a sibling or setting the table for dinner. Have him collect spare change from the sofa or play with a special toy while you are on the phone. You are giving attention when you want to for things that will help you, rather than responding to behavioral challenges and demands from your small being.

4. Learn ways to give attention that are quick and can be done anywhere. A wink, a thumbs-up, or a big smile can go a long way toward making your child feel that you care. Find a small signal that doesn't distract your entire family or rhythm of activity. Use this signal to communicate to your small being that you see him and are paying attention. Providing this type of attention countless times throughout the day may keep the challenging behavior away.
5. Proximity is powerful. If your small being wants lots of face time, have him sit near you. Just being close provides a level of attention that can keep challenging behavior at bay.
6. Once the demanding, attention-seeking behavior decreases and you are giving your child attention all the time on your own schedule and as a result of good behavior, start to *slowly* decrease the frequency of attention you provide. Slowness is the key. Once you are in control of when you dole out attention and your small one feels confident that attention is coming, you can start to change the frequency. Go slow so that problem behaviors do not come back. Only increase the time between reinforcements by minutes each week.

My craniosacral-therapy teacher used many of the strategies that were outlined above. An awkward pause set in after I asked him my question and he told me he needed a moment. I thought maybe I should just leave, but before I could do so, he took my hand and we walked to a table together. Once we sat down, he dropped my hand and filed away his papers. He then stood up, picked up my hand again, and walked over to one of the class assistants to speak about what was happening in the next section of class. Then he walked to a quiet corner of the room and motioned for me to sit down. He thanked me for my patience and said he could now give me his full attention. Throughout this series of interactions, I felt that my teacher cared. I was happy to wait for his attention.

Sometimes, giving someone all the attention the person needs in a particular moment has nothing to do with giving him or her all of our attention immediately. Start to enjoy the clear rules you create with your family around attention, and have fun getting them invested in the process.

The Smallest Step

Be clear in your language regarding attention. Speak with purpose because your words matter. If you say you cannot talk, don't. If you say you will answer, make sure you do so.

NOTES

Scenario 6:

He Acts Helpless

Dr. Marcie's Journey

You'll recognize this small being right away by your level of frustration. You *know* he is big enough and capable enough to do the task at hand, but he acts like he can't do it. You notice that he has this tendency especially when you ask him to clean up, stand up, sit down, throw out garbage, or tie his shoes. A few years ago, I guided a mother through a technique that required her small being to complete the tasks he already knew how to do. It was summer, and I had a home session scheduled with the family. We decided to meet at the park since the weather was so nice and one of the behaviors the family wanted support with was his interactions with peers. While I had never seen him at the park before, this child had seen me in his home and in his classroom several times. My job was to observe this particular small being's behavior at the park so that I could make suggestions for change to his parents as well as his teachers. Once I observe for a bit, I often step in to do some real-life skill building.

When I walked into the park, Ben, the child I was meeting, made it appear that he did not recognize me. You may be thinking, "Maybe he didn't see you," but he looked right at me as I stood just three feet from where he was playing. This was immediately a signal to me, as I was working closely with him and his family. At his school a few days before, I remember that he had easily used my name and was quite responsive to my directives.

Today Ben acted very differently toward me. He looked up when I walked over, saw me, and then went back to his sand-castle building. I said hello to his mother, put my things down, then walked over and said hello to Ben. He greeted me in return, but as if to a stranger. I sat on a nearby bench and continued watching his behavior.

During a lull in sandbox activity, I went over to him again and asked him what my name was. He said, "I don't know." "What's my name?" I asked again. He said he did not know. We went back and forth twenty-three times. I thought, "Maybe he really does not recognize me." I gave him some clues about who I was—that I saw him on Tuesday at school, we played *Guess Who?* during free play, and I helped pick out books to be read for the class. "I don't know," was still his answer. After seven more "I don't know" responses, I decided to give him my name. "My name is Dr. Marcie." I paused while he looked at me. "What's my name?"

He looked at me and said, "I don't know." I realized that he was not helpless or confused. This was purposeful behavior!

What This Means for Your Family

Acting helpless and being helpless are two different things. *Being* helpless means that the child is not able to complete the task at hand. When this is the case, you need to adjust your expectations. Age-appropriate, developmentally appropriate, and individualized needs all need to be taken into consideration when considering a small being's capabilities.

Acting helpless means that the small being in question *can* complete a task but chooses not to. Once you identify that this is the case, you can address and change the behavior. When you are met with a helpless response from your small being, first ask yourself, "Can my child physically and mentally do what you are asking him to do?" In many situations, the answer is no. Asking a three-year-old to sit through a forty-five-minute dinner full of adult conversation without moving is unrealistic. Asking a four-year-old to not run down the sidewalk—ever—is also unrealistic.

Curiosity is part of what makes children *children*. It's a beautiful thing and a very distracting tendency. With time, children learn to maintain focus while preserving their curiosity. Understand that some small beings develop faster than others in this area. Impulse control is something we as a society struggle to maintain, and it would be unreasonable to expect such control from any small being. (As written, this is a misinterpretation of the proverb. The problem isn't throwing stones at glass houses. It's throwing stones at others while you yourself live in a glass house and thus could not survive a return volley of stones.) The desire to do what feels good in the moment is innate; think about how many times a day you check your text messages.

Your Small Steps

The starting point is to answer this question: Is my small being physically and mentally capable of doing what I'm asking him to do? If he is not, then I suggest checking your assumptions. How realistic are they? Remember, you can always adjust your expectations. If you find that your child can do more but is choosing not to, the goal is to determine how to get him to do things independently.

When I realized that Ben was choosing to be helpless, I began working with his family and teachers on a plan. The goal was to keep him on task without individualized reminders and to have him make educated guesses when he wasn't sure. Also, we guided him to explain what he did not know using information he knew well. Eventually, and with persistent effort by his family and teachers, Ben started taking more initiative, acted less helpless, and used his problem-solving behaviors to complete tasks on his own.

Targeting Your Children's Behaviors

Start with one behavior: Write down the top ten behaviors that you would like your child to do independently and determine which one you think would have the most impact in your family.

Then, pick three things that would effectively transform your home if all members did them the first time you asked. Circle, star, or highlight them. Write them on a new piece of paper in clear, objective, observable, and measurable language.

For the next three days, make no changes. Watch and observe the three behaviors you want to target for independence. What do your children actually do? What do you do in response? Where do you see an opportunity for independence to be built into the routine?

Targeting Your Own Behaviors

Oftentimes, we (adults) are unwittingly part of the problem with undesirable behavior. As a parent, you are already amazing at multitasking. You monitor so many tasks at once, often many children at once, but there may be ways in which you create dependence without realizing it. This can happen when you are doing two things at once—for example, while giving directions to one child, you instinctively clean up a mess another created.

Your behavior must change first. If you want to build independence in your small ones, stop doing things for them. You tie shoes, help put on jackets, and zip up backpacks all without realizing it. When you stop doing these things for your children, they will have to do it all themselves.

Independence comes with age and capacity, so keep that in mind when outlining your steps for change. Make this transition gradually and systematically. Notice what your children expect you to do for them. Take one step back at a time from that support.

How to decrease support over time:

- Notice what support you provide unnecessarily and automatically; discontinue offering that help.

- Wait for your small being to ask for assistance.
- When someone asks you for help, have him try it once himself.
- If your child is unable to finish the task, offer a suggestion that will help him do it himself. Then let him try one more time.
- When your child asks for help again after that unsuccessful attempt, offer another suggestion. Then do it together.
- Continue this pattern every time your small being asks for help until the child is independent.

A Note About Consistency

Make sure to decrease your assistance over time in a step-by-step process. If you immediately stop giving all support, you will create a behavioral pushback and get negative behaviors in place of helpless behaviors. Adjust transition time as needed to make sure you are going at the right pace, but don't give up. You can do this! The most important thing is to continue decreasing support because if you go back to the old pattern you'll have to start all over.

The Smallest Step

Stop complaining about this behavior. Your shift in perspective will go further than you can imagine!

NOTES

Scenario 7:

She's Just Shy, Right?

Dr. Marcie's Journey

I once worked with a lovely six-year-old girl named Gita. My first interaction with her was at home. She was chatty and verbose. Gita had two siblings whom she loved to boss around. When her parents gave her a directive, she would immediately share an opinion or counteroffer. We all agreed that she would make a great lawyer one day. My task was to help this family move away from any back-and-forth with Gita by learning to use the power of their words.

Several weeks later, I did a school observation and was almost convinced that the Gita before me was a different small being. She made almost no eye contact with anyone, her voice was just above a whisper, and children took toys out of her hands without her protest. The teachers said that Gita was so shy that they had to let her go at her own pace. They did not push her, force her to answer questions, or engage in any activities in the classroom. I was shocked. Turns out this is also how she was during extended family gatherings, play dates outside of her house, and basically any situation outside of her home.

I set to work on trying to figure out how to bring out Gita's true personality in the classroom, as it was apparent that she was not an introvert at heart.

What This Means for Your Family

Adults are always trying to understand why a child is behaving in a certain way. When your child is exhibiting certain behaviors, do you lose hours of sleep trying to understand what is happening? If that time helps you find the solution, it is time well spent. Unfortunately, too often, the increased knowledge does not lead to a solution. For many parents, the hours of lost sleep result only in exhaustion with no clarity.

When trying to understand if your small being is shy or if it is a symptom of a behavioral challenge, the most frequent answer is that it does not matter. Being shy is never a problem. Antisocial or defiant behavior that sometimes *comes from shyness* is a problem. The goal is never to change anyone's personality, but extreme shyness can lead to negative behavioral patterns.

The line between shyness as a personality trait and shyness as a behavior is in the defiance that lies beneath the action. Being shy or an introvert is beautiful and many people who are happy and thriving in life identify that way. There is no problem with that. It is a perfect part of who someone is, so there is no need to change it if it makes for a happy life.

Regardless of where the timid behavior comes from, you need to address it when it prevents your child from interacting with others, including answering teachers and family friends, or if negatively impacting her friendships.

Your Small Steps

Think about when your small beings exhibit shy behavior. What do they exactly do that is shy? What do their behaviors objectively look like? Which of the behaviors are negative? Write these down. Making this distinction allows you to celebrate the personality traits that make your small beings unique, but address behaviors that will challenge their happiness. These include those that restrict her capacity to maintain friendships and/or her ability to perform functions in the "outside world."

Now that you are clear on what behaviors you are working to change, find a couple of situations that will stretch your child out of her comfort zone. Make gentle expansions; you don't want to encourage her to do something that will be too big of a step. Remember, it is small steps that lead to big behavior change. Model the behavior you want to see, and let her know that she can do it, too. Then set a rule that she must exhibit a certain behavior on a regular basis.

From my observations of Gita, I knew she had moments of shy behavior, although she was not a shy person. Just like I would for a child who was being disruptive, I created expectations for her behavior. While timid behavior is less of a challenge for the family, it is just as much of a challenge for the small being. After some convincing, I got the family and teachers on board with my plan. It did require the family to ask their friends to participate. Sometimes making change for your small being will need to include people outside of your immediate family. Be willing to ask those around you for help and support for the benefit of your child.

The first step was for the teachers or family friends to ask Gita a closed-ended question so that she only had to answer with a few words. Once she was comfortable, they moved on to open-ended questions, which required more creativity and independent answers. Previously, if Gita did not answer within a few moments, adults around her would move on, which allowed Gita to dodge a response. Now, at every questioning stage, the adults waited until Gita gave them the answer.

At home, I advised Gita's parents to only give her one option; an argument was not possible because there were no options to argue about. The parents stood firm with their decision, and after some resistance, Gita understood the rules. Please note that she was encouraged to use her debating prowess when she was not wielding it as a defiant behavior. We want to encourage all small beings to speak their mind, but not to do so in a way that makes life difficult for everyone.

I also advised Gita's parents to stop stepping in with other adults when Gita was not responding. When she was quiet and not answering, often her parents would answer for her. They thought they were making it easier for her. In reality, they were just making it easier for her to not answer. Part of Gita learning to engage with other adults necessitated her parents to stop supporting her when they knew she could answer herself. It builds independence, even though it was challenging for her parents to just wait for her answer.

After four months of deliberate work with Gita, the boisterous girl existed at home, in school, and on the playground. It was quite the transformation!

"Say Hi to a Friend" Strategy

Small beings are often identified as shy simply because they do not say hello to their friends. If you determine that a certain small being is not doing this for behavioral reasons or as a personality trait, then make a rule that she has to say hi to one friend each morning. The gesture could be as small as a wave or handshake, or as large as three verbal sentences.

Once she greets one friend daily for about a week, ask her to greet two friends. If your small being is consistent with that request, ask her to verbally say hello to at least one friend and greet two others. Keep increasing the required interactions until her shyness is no longer a challenging behavior. You will start to notice a positive change in the quality of her friendships as she gives attention to more people every day.

Creating gentle gradations is the key to shifting any timid behavior. Use it in all your behavioral plans. It is always the small steps that add up and make a big difference.

The Smallest Step

Get clarity on the behavior that is detrimental to happiness. Stop making excuses for the seemingly shy behaviors when they take away from the happiness of your small being.

NOTES

Do More, Actions Count

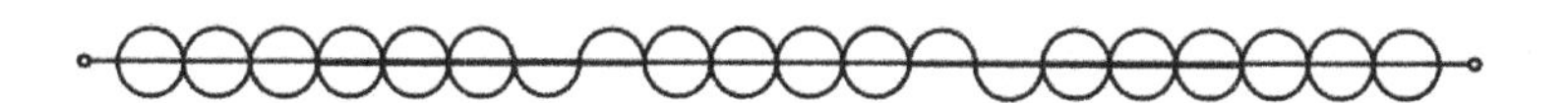

PART TWO

We've all heard that actions speak louder than words. In my practice, I use the phrase "do more: actions count" as a reminder to my clients to stop repeating themselves and take action. Do you repeat yourself frequently? Are you frustrated that your small beings are not listening to you the first time, or the thirty-fifth time, you say something? Do you tell your children that you will do something but often forget because there are so many things you need to be doing? All of these instances are indicators that your actions need to become the focus to change behavior.

In Part 1 you learned about the importance of your words. It is critical that you speak with purpose. But sometimes words are not enough. Your power resides in actions; actions teach your children to listen. Actions translate the meaning of your words to your small beings. Words alone are not enough. It is what you *do* that changes everything!

In order for small beings to listen the first time, you need to say things once, then take action. This is best demonstrated in examples, rather than explained with more words. You might say to your child, "Time to put on your shoes." Do not repeat yourself when your child (let's call her Stephanie), does not come right away, especially if you know she rarely comes when you call her to put on her shoes (even if she knows you are going somewhere super fun). Immediately after you say the direction, take action: walk over to her, take her hand, and say, "Let's get our shoes on together." By taking action, you avoid the frustration of repeating yourself and being ignored. When you consistently do this, Stephanie will learn to respond the first time you issue a directive. You taught her that you say things once and then take action.

You may find that you repeat your message multiple times when your small being exhibits bad behavior. Many adults use this technique, as if when a small being did not listen the first time, she might listen the seventh time. In moments like these, words alone will seldom change your small being's behavior, as this small being has already learned that she does not need to listen to your words. She has learned that you will repeat yourself and nothing more.

If you are curious as to why your words are not enough, especially during a tantrum, it is because logic and reasoning do not function during intense emotions that come with intense behavior. Think about a time you were upset, perhaps a time your boss gave you some feedback in a less than kind way. Did you hear every word that was said to you in that disciplinary moment? Nope. The same thing happens with your small beings. If your goal is to change behavior, you need to stop talking so much and start doing more.

The only messages that will be understood will come through your actions. As you are taking steps in your plan to change challenging behavior, try talking about what you are doing clearly and in action-based terms. For example, you can say, "Now we are putting on our shoes." If you continue to talk to Stephanie about why it is so important for her to put on her shoes, how she knows better, et cetera, she will never listen. Her behavior is not likely to change based on repetitive verbal instruction. If you give the direction and then *walk* Stephanie over to where her shoes are, now her behavior has changed. Your words of comfort and discipline are well meaning, but they do not create the behavioral change that you and your children need.

The action-based model is processed on a different level than the verbal-based model. When you are thoughtful and specific about what you do, your small being's behavior will follow suit. Consistency in your actions facilitates trust between you and your children. You are teaching them that their negative behaviors will not change your actions—a very powerful lesson!

Transitions at school are often a time when children's behavior can go awry. Here is another specific situation where I outline how to shift the dynamic with your actions. Again, executing this concept is better done with actions than words.

At the end of the school day, your child generally plays independently until you arrive to take her home. Your small being, Stephanie, usually plays nicely until you get there. As soon as you walk in the door, you begin to hear from the teacher all about Stephanie's progress. Stephanie starts yelling for your attention from across the room. While your child keeps shouting, the teacher keeps calling back not to interrupt and asks you a rather loaded question about your daughter's behavior at home.

This is the perfect situation in which to use your actions to change the behavioral dynamic. You want to set up the situation for all parties to be successful. When you arrive at her classroom, call your daughter over. She will eagerly come and be happy to comply. Give her a direction such as, "Give me a hug and tell me about one thing that happened today." Stephanie will thus receive your attention right away. The teacher will have to comply as well, since you will not speak with her until your daughter is finished talking about her achievement. If the teacher indicates that she has a question for you, turn to your child to let her know that she needs to play quietly for a few minutes while you talk with her teacher.

I am a fan of setting a timer as it keeps me honest in saying that I'll only be a few minutes. If the teacher has more questions than the allotted time, that might mean you should set up a meeting. If your small being comes over and tries to interrupt, simply point to the timer and keep talking. This part takes a bit of getting used to, but you can do it. Convince the teacher that she needs to stay in the conversation without breaking away to explain to your child what is happening. You already explained, and now is the time to reinforce the explanation with action.

I have used this process many times with parents and teachers and it works like a charm! You don't need to over explain or ask your children to wait over and over and over again. Show them, and it will happen.

Action Steps for "Do More: Actions Count"

1. Notice your actions. Notice when your words could use a physical follow-through.
2. Observe the small moments when you are not using your actions; this often happens when you use too many words. There's no judgment here, only simple observation.
3. Notice the behavior of your small beings around you when you are using words over actions. Is it

behavior you want to continue or behavior you would like to change?

4. If it is behavior you want to maintain, great! Keep up those actions. If it is behavior you want to change, then consider what behavior you prefer instead. Get really clear on what that behavioral interaction looks like and write it down.
5. Write down why this behavior is important. Why is this particular behavioral shift critical?
6. Begin to take small steps toward focusing on taking intentional actions rather than just speaking. Take it one moment at a time when practicing this principle.
7. Celebrate each moment that you take action. Notice the behavioral response for your small beings. Celebrate with them when they have the behavior you desire.
8. Keep taking small steps until you naturally follow up your words with actions a majority of the time. It is an ongoing practice for us all!

Now that you understand how this rule can be applied, let's explore some specific scenarios where "do more: actions count" can be an automatic part of your parenting and a key you may use to unlock outstanding behavior.

Scenario 8: She Can't Tell Me Why She Did It

Dr. Marcie's Journey

After snowstorms in New York City there are often large piles of dirty snow in the streets that seem to stay there for ages. They remain for weeks or months until the weather is warm enough to melt them away. About a week after a blizzard, I was walking down the street. As I passed the bus stop, I watched a two-year-old (we'll call her Faith) reach out for a handful of snow as she passed a snow bank. I smiled at how kids find fun in the snow, no matter what shape it's in.

Her mom must have seen the same move, but it was obvious she felt very differently about it. My guess was that her thought was more along the lines of, "How gross! How could a child of mine ever do that?" It was an educated guess at her thought based solely on her facial expression. The confirmation came when she started screaming at little Faith. "Why? Why would you do that?

The snow is so dirty! You do not touch dirty snow! What were you thinking?"

This little girl was very smart. She did not say a word. Granted, this made her mom even angrier, but Faith wasn't in a position to reveal her honest answer: "because snow is fun." Perhaps she did not have the words to say that even if she wanted to.

During my time with parents and teachers, I see countless adults ask small beings why they behave in a certain way. Learning to drop this question and respond with actions instead will give you the space to solve more behavioral problems.

What This Means for Your Family

Humans are curious by nature; we simply want to understand what is going on around us. Because of this trait, we have a tendency to believe that when we understand the reasons behind a problem, the problem may be easily solved. Werner Erhard, a critical thinker and author, once said, "Understanding is the booby prize." Trying to understand your child's behavior will lead you down a frustrating path. The reality is that you can create behavior change without understanding the why behind it.

Now, stop and think for a moment about how your small beings must feel upon hearing a question about their actions that begins with "why." They know they did something wrong and now have to explain it to a big being who is disappointed, angry, or frustrated. Just the thought of being in the situation makes my heart pound! When I was in that situation as a small being, I remember often choosing to make up the answer I thought they wanted. Didn't you?

In the moments right after a negative behavior, most people cannot articulate why they did what they did, even if they have an intellectual understanding. Small beings are no exception. They give you the answer they think you're looking for and hope that the conversation ends as soon as possible.

We often ask small beings "why" questions right after they make a mistake. Not only are they feeling bad about their action, but now they have to justify it. That is a tall order for your small being and quite unrealistic.

Dropping this question is important for your child's development in the following ways:

- You are frustrating yourself. A lot of times, you already know the answer. When your child cannot respond you get frustrated. Also, why waste time asking a question that you know has no good answer? When you are annoyed, you can't help your child as well as you usually can.
- Asking "why" teaches small beings to disconnect from their actual emotional state. They start to try to figure out what you want them to say rather than focusing on what really happened. This is the beginning of a manipulating and pleasing behavior that is never beneficial.
- The question creates the opportunity for your children to lie and be rewarded for lying. If they tell you the truth, they may get into more trouble. If they lie, they may avoid punishment.

- It doesn't solve the problem. Understanding "why" does not teach the small ones how to do anything better next time. When you focus on understanding the emotional state and reasoning of the moment, you miss a valuable teaching moment that will change behavior.

Your Small Steps

During family sessions, I have witnessed a lot of back-and-forth between parents and children about behavioral reasoning. After the moment of conversation, I will usually ask the parent to answer the question from the perspective of their child. The parent will always give me a fairly accurate reply. I bet if I asked the mom from the story in the beginning of the chapter about why her daughter went to touch the snow, she would have a good answer for me as well.

So why are you bothering to ask the question you already know the answer to? By making these queries, you are setting up your small beings to make up an answer they know you would prefer to the truth. Your goal should be to never create a situation where it is best for your child to lie.

Stop asking "why" no matter how tempting it is!

Start talking about what physically happened—the actions! Then you can have a conversation about what actions would be better to take next time. Let's start with asking our small beings to control their bodies before we start asking them to control their emotions.

Here is a model script to help you change your line of questioning:

You: What happened here?
Small Being: I don't know.
You: Can you tell me what you did?
Small Being: I was playing with that toy.
You: That sounds like fun, but your brother is crying.
Small Being: He wanted to play with it, too.
You: Oh. So, he is crying because you won't let him play with the toy.
Small Being: I had it first.
You: I see. What can you do next time so that your brother does not cry?
Small Being: I don't want to share. I can give it to him when I'm done.
You: That sounds like a great plan.

Yes, this is a very simplified version, and your small being may not always have such clear answers. You will need to modify the script as you go through the situation, but maintain two basic principles:

1. Your language centers around taking action.
2. You use positive language; there is no judgment or blame. This allows the conversation to be proactive and a teaching moment!

The Smallest Step

Notice how often you ask "why," and think about the quality of the answers you receive. Observation alone can shift behavior.

NOTES

Scenario 9: He Answers With a Blank Stare

Dr. Marcie's Journey

One of my seven-year-old clients, Malik, has oppositional defiance disorder (ODD). Because of the disorder, he was a master at answering questions with a blank stare. During any given session, he would burst into my office with a story, like how his Lego project fell apart or about an adventure with a friend over the weekend. But when he finally finished talking and I asked him a question, he would show a very different side of himself. Malik responded to simple queries like, "How are you?" with a blank stare. Invitations for participation like, "What do you want to do?" were also met with a blank stare. Unless he wanted to talk, Malik did not talk.

My frustration level went through the roof, but I did not give up. I kept asking the same question, in the same language, until he answered. Sometimes it took half the session. Mind you, his parents were in the room with us. Do you know how strange it is to ask a small being the same question fifty times while another adult watches? His mother or father occasionally tried to interrupt, and after my brief hand signals showing "stop asking me right now" didn't work, I simply ignored them and kept repeating the same question. It was a fascinating dynamic. Eventually we made progress using the techniques that I outline in this scenario.

What This Means for Your Family

This behavior is my absolutely biggest pet peeve. Luckily, I have the training and experience to keep my emotional response in check. You've probably noticed that certain behaviors really get under your skin. It is important to note which behaviors these are for you so that you can proceed with caution. Do not overreact to your child because of your own disposition.

Behaviors like Malik's can be confusing. Did the small being not hear you? Does he think you are talking to someone else? Did he suddenly forget how to talk? Your small being is just looking for a reaction. He does not even attempt to answer. What are you supposed to do with that?

Your child is not answering because he doesn't know that it is required of him. He knows that if he waits long enough, someone else will answer, you will give up, or a distraction will occur. Your child might be defiant, a perfectionist, shy, or easily distracted. Knowing why he stares back when you ask a question can be interesting, but it does not excuse the behavior. Your small being needs to answer, and it is your job to teach him to do so.

Teach your children to take a guess any time they don't know the answer. I have found that more often than not, small beings guess the right answer.

Your Small Steps

Teach your small ones that they must answer your questions. Over time, they have come to understand that answering your questions with a blank stare is acceptable. You did not mean for this to happen, but it did. Now you must remedy it.

The solution is not to explain to them why it is important that they answer the question. Chances are they already know. It is not to ask the question in a different way. Chances are they understood your language. It is to show them the importance of answering by making them answer your question.

When I was relentless in repeating my question to Malik, he eventually realized that he had to answer! He gave me the shortest answers possible: "okay," "fine," or "dunno." At first, I was thrilled with these short answers, especially when he gave them the first time I asked. Gradually, I changed my expectation for him to include more information. Eventually, we saw that he was capable of giving complete, polite answers. It was a slow but satisfying shift.

Teaching your small being can be both simple and difficult. It takes the will to stick to your guns while the rest of your life waits. It is worth the effort and can be a lesson for all of your family! Remember this in the most challenging moments.

If you are committed, here is a script:

- Identify that you are asking your child a question by using his name at the beginning of the question.
- State the question clearly.
- Wait while making eye contact with your child. Wait past your comfort level.
- After a full sixty seconds, use your child's name and ask the exact same question again. Do not include new language or phrasing.
- Wait while making eye contact with your child for another full sixty seconds.
- Keep this going until he makes some sort of response.

If another family member offers to help, remind that person that it is not his or her turn and that you are waiting for this participator family member to give an answer. Say this simply, clearly, and politely.

Most children give no response because they have learned that if they wait long enough, you will eventually give them the answer or move on to something else. Teaching them the need to try is critical to engaging them. Intentionally be repetitive and boring in your responses. Do not use inflection or signal that you are trying to convince them to answer.

You have several options if your child says, "I don't know":

1. Thank him for answering, and ask another family member the same question.
2. Request that he take one guess. You can explain that, "The great thing about a guess is you don't have to be right. You simply need to think and say your first

thought." For the perfectionist-minded child, this comment takes the pressure off being correct.

This process is not a one-shot deal. You'll need to repeat it over and over so that your small being will learn that he must answer when asked a question. Have patience as you put this plan into action. Once learned it will be a solidified skill that was certainly worth the patience and attention.

The Smallest Step

Start asking your child who does not answer if he wants to answer. Do not require him to respond to your question. By giving him this choice, it puts him in a position where he is responding no matter what he decides to say or do.

NOTES

Scenario 10:

She Never Says "Please" or "Thank You"

Dr. Marcie's Journey

I sometimes feel kids today speak a different language than I do. One day I was on the subway, when a group of twelve-year-olds coming home from school boarded the train. They were loud and laughing. Overall, while disruptive, they were having a great time together. It was rather amusing, at least to me.

They surprised me with the language they used. Their words were not explicitly rude, but they were not kind or polite either. I did not hear compliments or pleasantries. I kept listening, wondering if were they actually being rude to each other or if it was their language and tone that made them seem that way.

Their actions told a different story. From their behavior, they were clearly enjoying themselves and happy. They were very respectful of each other and even more so to those around them. When the doors opened at a crowded stop, one gently pushed another one out of the way of a fellow passenger getting off the train. One member of the group started singing, and her friends apologized to nearby strangers for her blaring voice. These actions were considerate, even when the language was not.

However, a man further down the subway car asked them to "settle down." This publicly challenged the almost teens' views of themselves. I was on the edge of my seat, waiting for what might come next.

What This Means for Your Family

In your family, *you* make the rules. If you make using "please" and "thank you" part of your family culture, then your children will use those words every day. Children won't, however, naturally use these words without the right model. That's okay, as your job is to teach them beneficial skills and manners. Spend some time teaching how, when, and why to use "please" and "thank you." It is the small stuff that makes the biggest impact.

It's also important to be clear with children about your expectations. Do you have family or house rules or a description of what behavior is appropriate? If not, create a list and post it in a frequently passed part of your home. If you already have this up and running, pat yourself on the back!

Prompts are necessary so that small beings use "please" and "thank you" on a regular basis. Over time, these words will become part of a child's natural language. Using prompts does not mean you put the words in a small being's mouth or only remind the child after he or she forgot; it means that you give him or her a reminder and your small being must use independent thinking to remember the full meaning.

You may need to focus your family on politeness for a period of time in order to make a substantial change. Your daily focus on the behavior will help. Like all behavioral shifts, it requires consistency. Taking the time to teach your children these skills, however, is a gift that each of your children will carry with them for the rest of their lives. The effort is certainly worth it!

Your Small Steps

Back to the kids on the subway. When I last mentioned them, they were loud, one was singing, and a man on the other side of the car yelled, "Settle down!" I sat on the edge of my seat. This is the New York City subway; you never know what is going to happen!

One of the girls looked at him and said, dripping with sarcasm, "You could have said 'please.'" Then the group calmed down a bit. Fascinating! These kids showed they knew how to be respectful even when they did not sound that way. They wanted respect but had no idea that they were disrespectful.

If the man on the subway wanted to be instructive rather than punitive, he could have taken a different approach. He could have gotten up, walked over to them, and asked in a calm voice, "Do you mind quieting down, please?" Notice that in this new dynamic, the man treats them as equal human beings. Let this serve as a great reminder that if we want others to act in a certain way, we just need to show them how to do it. Let actions lead.

I wonder if your kids have had similar experiences. When you do not expect your child to say "please" and "thank you," your child will most likely not use those words. They know what these words mean and when to use them, but they don't, which is frustrating for you. When I am with my clients, who know that they must always speak politely to me, parents think that I cast a magic spell over the families. There is no magic, I promise! It's simply that my expectations are crystal clear.

You can start creating a polite home environment by using pleasantries yourself. Say "please" when you ask your child for something; say "thank you" if your child hands you the object requested. Your children will notice and may start to imitate your behavior without any direct instruction.

You may also integrate this into your family rules or guidelines. Make it very clear. Protocol that states "be polite" is rather ambiguous. What does "polite" look like in terms of actual behavior? Be more specific. For example, write "Be sure to always say please and thank you." Review this rule, as well as your other family rules, with your children on a daily basis, as a constant reminder of their importance within (and outside of) your home.

Use your actions to best integrate this rule into your family culture. Here are some guided examples:

- **Parent-Initiated Interaction:**
  Each time you hand your child something (a snack, her coat, a book, etc.) look at her and say, "Here you go, [name of your child]," with a smile. Then keep hold of that item until she says "Thank you." No prompts. Just wait. The first few times you do this, she will be very confused, then she will start problem solving by pulling harder or saying, "I got it." Other family members around

the child will watch and learn by what you do next. Wait for their words of gratitude. When your child says them, immediately let go of the item and say, "You're welcome." The structure and routine of the language helps solidify the use of these polite words. Do not lecture the child at any point; use your actions to guide her response.

- **Child-Requested Initiation:**
  When your child asks you for something she needs, you have a golden opportunity to teach her manners. For example, when your small being says, "Can I have an apple for a snack?" wait for the "please." Keep looking at her so she knows you heard her. Don't say a word, and don't move on to something else. Just wait. Your child will start to problem solve. "Well, can I?" Keep waiting. Maybe you glance at the rules list as a clue. Let her figure it out, and when she finally says, "Can I have an apple for a snack, please?" you can respond with, "Of course, thank you for asking." Even when the request is so good that you are tempted to quickly say sure, don't do it if your focus is on teaching politeness.

Whether you or your child starts an interaction, the universal expectation should be that it is a polite exchange. The more frequently you use these techniques, the sooner words of gratitude will be a natural part of your family vocabulary.

The Smallest Step

Stop lecturing about politeness! Either take steps to change the etiquette in your family or do not complain that your small beings are not polite.

NOTES

Scenario 11: He Never Stops Whining

Dr. Marcie's Journey

My mother never put up with whining or being interrupted by me or my sister. If she were on a phone call and I asked her a question, she would look at me and respond, "Is someone bleeding or dead?"

I can't remember a time when I answered yes to that question. So I always just shook my head and said, "No, but—"

She would then cut me off and say, "Then you can't interrupt. I will talk with you when I am off the phone," and she would go back to her call. It was effective; I rarely interrupted her on the phone. I also learned the power of problem solving without my mother's help, which has proven to be a helpful life skill.

Usually when your small being is whining, he is not in a calm mental state. Staying strong in your actions is crucial. My mom would say, "I don't listen to whining," and walk away every single time and without hesitation.

My sister and I did not use this behavior often because it did not work—ever!

Please know that my mother was always very loving toward us. At other times, she would take lots of time to talk with us and help us and support our growth. I would come to her with a problem and we would solve it together. When it came to whining or interrupting her, however, she did not budge. She was consistent in implementing her two rules and so we knew to abide by them.

There are many solid behavioral techniques similar to those my mother used. Read on to find out how you can apply them in your family.

What This Means for Your Family

The simple truth about whining is this: if your child whines as a regular form of communication, he does so because it works! Whining usually results in a favorable experience that he likes and wants to continue. If it did not, he would stop whining.

It's that simple. Behaviors occur for only a few reasons, or *functions*: desire for attention, desire for escape, because it feels good, or due to a medical condition. When your child is interrupting or whining, chances are that he is doing so for attention. When you give him what he wants after whining, he will continue the undesirable behavior.

You'll notice that the behaviors that persist or increase are the ones that get enjoyable results. Behaviors that disappear do so as a result of outcomes that are not desired or enjoyable. Of course, enjoyment is subjective. You might wonder what is enjoyable to your small being about, for example, your raised voice and obvious agitation. If he is receiving attention, he may be accomplishing his goal, no matter how it looks or feels to you. It is not for you to judge whether his perspective is "normal" or "correct." Simply take it as it is. He enjoys the response you give. You are giving him what he wants. It is likely that he uses whining in other parts of his life, as it is often a cry for attention and control. Your small being knows that when he uses his regular voice, he does not get what he wants quickly, if at all. Like all behaviors, this one was built over time and is reinforced by the environment.

Here's where you come in. The behavior in your home and family is in your control. While it is tempting to blame teachers or friends for your child's whining habit, you are a significant participant in your child's behaviors. You must always remember that your small beings are smart; they understand many common rules of engagement, meaning which tactics work for specific people.

We all engage in certain actions hoping for specific outcomes based on experience. This is what controls all of our behavior. Our small ones are no exception and neither are you. Think about the world's largest coffee chain, Starbucks. It is incredibly popular because the result of a customer's interaction is very similar across all locations. You can go into any Starbucks, anywhere in the world, and get the same vanilla latte. People choose what they know will work, whether it is attention from their parents or a caffeine fix from Starbucks.

Patterns of interaction create behavior. You are essentially rewriting that framework for a small being, so it will take persistent and consistent effort to change it. Over time, you have the ability to show your whining child that his usual path will no longer get him where he wants to go with you. He must find another way to get to his ultimate goal.

Your Small Steps

My mother did not give me the attention I craved when I would whine and interrupt her, so I learned that I *could* get attention for good behavior (kind, polite, appropriate communication) and *could not* get attention for behavior that was irritating, annoying, or frustrating. She remained steadfast during every moment of the negative behavior.

This is the model you must provide to your children:

1. Stop providing attention for whining behavior.
2. Start providing attention for good behavior (proper, kind, polite appropriate) communication.

It sounds simple because it is! Use your actions over your words on a consistent basis, and you will shift the negative behavior. There is one addition to these steps regarding *how* the behavior will evolve.

Behavior is not a vacuum; it's very important to provide a replacement behavior for the one you have eradicated. If you do not teach a replacement behavior, your child will find a substitute that is worse than whining. Make sure all small beings in your family are clear about what to do in order to get your attention. These include tapping you on the shoulder, asking a sibling for help, and simply waiting. When small beings choose more destructive methods, continue to ignore them if possible.

Here is the plan:

1. Let your children know that there is a new focus on voice and volume. You will be teaching them to speak in their beautiful, full voice. Whispers, whining, and yelling (you can throw in this negative vocal behavior or focus on one manner of speaking at a time) will not be answered or in any way acknowledged from that point forward.
2. Plan on reminding your family of this rule three times a day. It must be enough times that your children remember but not so many that it creates frustration. It is important to keep reminders going past the end of the behavior you are changing. If whining is an ongoing problem with multiple family members (perhaps yourself included), you may want to remind everyone before each section of your day.
3. The first time a child whines or yells say, "Please try that sentence again." If you have very young children you may simply want to say, "Try again."
4. If your child does so in a better way, fantastic! If not, it is your turn to put your words into action and ignore the whining.
5. If other people (especially considering that you often parent in public) see the interaction and question your behavior, tell them of your new rule. "We are working on talking in our regular voices. As soon as [name of your child] asks in his regular voice, I will be happy to answer." This helps those around you feel good about the intervention.
6. Keep the reminders going for two weeks after all whining behavior is gone. Then reduce the

reminders to just once a day. If the peace continues, reduce the reminders just to the time when you are reviewing family rules.

The Smallest Step

Celebrate when your child who usually whines speaks in his regular voice. If you treat it as expected behavior rather than an improvement, you are shortchanging your child and yourself.

NOTES

Scenario 12: She Knows Better

Dr. Marcie's Journey

Many of my clients have trouble focusing. Some of them have a diagnosis of attention disorders, and some do not. Deja, with whom I worked from age four through age seven, was diagnosed with attention-deficit/hyperactivity disorder (ADHD) midway through our work together.

Her teachers complained that she had trouble sitting in class. Her parents found the same thing at home. She easily became antsy and then found a way to disrupt the classroom, meal time, or quality family time. Her parents hired me because she was being sent out of the classroom more and more and was creating chaos at home.

After one school observation, I knew the motivation for Deja's behavior: she liked going to the office. When I did the home session, I noticed the same thing: she preferred the conversation about her bad behavior over playing games or eating with her family. Acting out resulted in an enjoyable experience. She didn't mind getting into trouble because the office was quiet and being sent to her room was, too. These quiet spaces helped her calm down. Also, every grown-up who went in and out of the office stopped and talked with her. That attention was like candy for this little being.

I spoke at length with her parents, teachers, and the school administrators. They all expressed frustration with Deja because the conversation had already been had with her about asking for a break when she needed one. Deja told them all that she understood. She knew better, so why did she continue to act out?

This is a rather common situation. Knowing and actually doing are two different things. Communication breakdown often happens around behaviors like nudging, hitting, and interrupting that sometimes occur after a child is distracted.

When I first started working with four-year-old Deja, she had a tendency to hit other children even though she certainly knew the rules. Like many preschoolers, she walked around saying, "No hitting allowed!" or "No yelling!" She also monitored other children's behaviors, and when they were out of line, she would directly tell them. We worked a lot on making sure she knew the difference between a teacher's job and a small being's job.

The solution to the discrepancy in understanding was incredibly simple, but first let's understand a bit more about the causes.

What This Means for Your Family

It's amazing how something may be cognitively clear to us, yet in the moment of application, one fails to put words into action. Everyone has had that experience; it is what makes us human. Picture a time in your life when you did not do what you know was the right thing to do, but could not help yourself. This memory helps you have more empathy for your children. We've all been there!

One relevant example for many adults is related to food and exercise. The body thrives with certain foods and needs a certain amount of exercise to feel good. We all share this knowledge, but do most people follow healthy recommendations?

Knowing what is right and putting that knowledge into action are two different things. The first requires simply learning about an idea. The second requires you to apply that idea. Behavioral challenges rarely stem from a lack of knowledge, but rather an incapacity to convert that knowledge into action.

This is what is happening with your child right now. She *does* know better. She does *not* know how to put that knowledge into action. Stop blaming her for not doing what she knows, and instead reframe the situation to recognize that this is a teaching moment for a skill this small being needs to learn.

Deja required the same game plan. I noticed that when she hit other people, she always looked shocked. When I asked her if she hit, she always admitted it. She was able to articulate that she felt she was "bad" and that everyone was disappointed in her. She had such clarity, but she simply could not stop herself.

I asked her parents and teachers to give her reminders. Initially, they all laughed. She knew the rules, so what was the point? I responded that Deja did not give herself reminders at the right time. She needed some help during the usual times that she had problem behavior.

Right before transitions and during long periods of unstructured play. The adults reminded Deja of the no-hitting rule every fifteen minutes. It worked like magic. This small being was suddenly able to control her hitting. She would be so proud of herself when she had not hit anyone during outdoor time. The intentional reminders at the right time went so far for her!

Your Small Steps

Create a proactive, rather than reactive, action plan. You want your child to be able to enact the knowledge that she already has!

It is vital to step in when your small being expresses a lack of hope of changing her behavior. She knows the rules, but just not how to apply them. You need to show her the way. Stop talking about the right choices, as she knows what those are. Instead, create situations where she can practice *making* the right choice. Provide support to ensure that it is a positive experience, so as to solidify the behavior. This needs to happen over and over again, not just one time for it to become a behavioral habit. It is the practice of the actions that makes the behavior change occur.

What does this look like exactly? Here is an example script you can use. Just make sure to tailor the details for your particular child:

When your small being wakes up in the morning, say to her, "Today is going to be a great day! You are going to listen and be focused all day. If you need a break, simply ask for it, and we will find a way to make it happen right away." Then, during each transition and right before you start a new activity, walk over to your child and with kindness say, "If you need a break, please just let me know."

A simple reminder makes it more likely that your small one will use this technique before problem behavior happens. When she does ask for a break, let her go. When she comes back, congratulate her for doing such a great job. Let her know how amazing she did.

With some smaller beings, you might have to take one or two additional steps:

- Step one: Start giving your child breaks. Have her go to her room for a quiet break that helps keep her calm.
- Step two: At the very first sign of disruptive behavior, walk over and ask your child if she needs a break. If the answer is yes, let her go, and let this be considered a success. Before she can take the break, have her ask for it. This will give her the experience of asking for a break and then getting it. Yes, it was prompted, but this one element can go a long way toward building independence.

After three successful days of immediate reminders, see if you can fade to one reminder at the beginning of each period.

After five successful days of reminders at the beginning of each period, try reducing the reminders to every other period. Keep on this schedule until the reminders are only once a day and then eventually fade them out completely.

You want to make sure that your child does not take too many breaks or purposely increase the frequency. Keep track of how many times she uses the privilege, and look for an increase in requests. If you start to see this pattern, you might want to give her a specific number of times that she can take a break in a day. Decrease that number as you see success, in the same way the number of reminders is reduced.

The Smallest Step

Keep focused on the actions. When you talk with your small one about her behavior, focus only on the actions that you saw happen; not the interpretation, reasoning, or feelings behind the actions.

NOTES

Scenario 13:

He's Just a Bad Kid

Dr. Marcie's Journey

The office phone for my private practice is like the Batphone for people who have tried the traditional options for changing a small being's behavior and nothing has worked. People tend to look outside of the conventional solutions as a last resort, so they'll call my practice, a group of nontraditional behavior specialists, when they don't know what else to do. Because of that pattern, I work with "bad kids" regularly. Parents are exasperated and teachers are wary of them. Turning these children's behavior around is my specialty.

In every school, there is a kid who gets a bad rap—one who is labeled a "bad kid." His past teachers warn upcoming teachers, and it feels as if even at the very start of the school year, he is not liked by his teachers.

Is this your child? Does it seem that no matter what happens, you just keep seeing signs that he is bad and that gets reinforced by everyone around you?

Because I have a collaborative practice, I take the time to speak with all therapists or teachers who work with a small being. Sometimes I receive a suggestion akin to, "Just give up. There's no hope for this child." This always shocks me; they're just kids! As a parent, I understand when you express such feelings. Yet hearing it from professionals is never acceptable.

One particular small being, Liam, was nine years old. He had not received an official diagnosis, but I suspected that someone could have labeled him with oppositional defiant disorder (ODD) or ADHD. When I started working with him, I happened to be in touch with the director of the preschool he attended. He was the middle child of his family, and the director saw all three children come through her school.

One day, while connecting with the director about another matter, I asked her, with his family's permission, about this particular small being. She took a deep breath and said that he was going to have a tough life because he was a bad seed. She started to recount some incidents that happened when he was in preschool. Wow, he really did sound like a bad seed!

I asked her one question at the end, "When was the last time you saw this small one?" She said it was when he graduated preschool four years ago. I was shocked that even though she had not seen him in four years, she was happy to share her thoughts about his future.

I thanked her for her thoughts, made some notes, and went on my way. Then I started to work with Liam, his family, and his current teachers to uncover a strategy to improve his behavior. I took all of the director's insights with a big grain of salt.

What This Means for Your Family

Can you imagine being this child? Just for one moment, take off the grown-up hat to visualize what it would be like to be the "bad kid." Everyone expects you to be in trouble. You feel your parents slowly begin to give up on you. All teachers and administrators watch you with suspicion, ready to jump at you with a reprimand.

How does that feel? The pressure is crushing. The looks are devastating. Because you're just a kid, you believe everyone is right and that you must be an awful kid. You might as well throw the rules aside, because that's what everyone expects of you.

If you're still not convinced that the "bad eggs" are affected by their troublemaking stigma, then consider my experience with nine-year-old Liam. When I asked him to tell me three things that were amazing in his life, he could not. When asked to name three things he did wrong that day, the list went on and on. He deeply internalized people's negative assumptions.

If you, as his parent, brace yourself for your child's behavior each and every day, then you're doomed to have a trying life together. When you hold expectations that your child will behave terribly, he will meet that expectation, because behavior is interactive and dynamic. To a certain degree we act in relationship to those around us. What you do as a parent will influence how your small one behaves. His behavior and what you know about him also influences how you behave. When you intentionally change these expectations for the positive, you will have an easier time shifting his behavior.

As a parent, it may be challenging to explain to his teachers what an amazing child he is when the behavior does not match. Part of your job, however, is to take care of your small beings. So, in addition to the ideas below, also consider how you interact with his teachers, and guide them to use the same small steps to help change your child's behavior.

Your Small Steps

In order to be effective, you need to both forget the past *and* be prepared in case it happens again!

Try to ignore the frustration and aggravation in the voices of relatives or opinionated friends. Pay attention to what your small being is actually saying and doing, *not* to what others may be saying about your small being, especially when there is a challenging situation. Don't automatically assume your child is in the wrong.

What if you were the one person who took the time to understand him? Behavior is communication of a need. Could you determine what your child truly needs and provide it before challenging behavior arises? With some careful preparation, you can!

More than anyone else in your family, this child needs your actions to speak louder than your words. You need to be impeccable with how you respond each and every time there is problem behavior. Make sure you are on top of your directions, and do what you say you will. No idle threats and no taking back stated consequences. Be strong, be clear, and put everything into action.

Many small beings determine what our expectations of them are through small behaviors we have, signals we give that show we expect a problem. Show him you expect difficulties, and you will certainly get them. Or, make it clear that you believe he can succeed and give him the step-by-step support to do so.

If you are clear, direct, and in control, you have a better chance of your child listening to you. You may be the one person who gets through. Be calm, cool, and collected. Forge a positive relationship with your child. Give him the chance to succeed because he can, and with your help, he will.

I needed to show Liam, my nine-year-old client, that he mattered. He was yearning for someone to tell him he could flourish and that there was good in him. The conversations about how he messed up needed to end, and there needed to be more talk about what he was doing well. I worked with all of the care providers in his life, and we shifted the dynamic in this manner. Liam changed his behavior with these adjustments. I was able to support changes in the boy's behavior that no one had previously succeeded in transforming simply because I showed him where the good in him was.

Your actions will determine your child's behavior. Here is your plan:

1. Listen to the teachers' insights. Ask objective questions about your child's behavior and how it was handled. You'll pull from this information an understanding of what worked and what did not work. Be aware of objective language versus subjective language.
2. Create a behavior plan for your child. How will you respond if you receive the same challenging behavior from last time?
3. Write down the behavior plan. Review it at least three times a week at the beginning of the day. The tools

will be fresh in your mind as your family gets the day started, and you will be prepared if anything occurs.

4. Keep an open mind. Believe that good behavior and a positive relationship are possible. Put this positive attitude into action by encouraging him and giving him small steps to success.
5. Find three small ways to compliment your child every day. Building a positive dynamic will be behaviorally beneficial in the future.
6. Know that you are on your way to changing your small being's behavior by putting all your ideas into positive action steps!

The Smallest Step

Believe that it is possible for your child to be different. Even this small mental shift will help you and your "problem" child flourish!

NOTES

Scenario 14: Her Teachers *Do Not* Care

Dr. Marcie's Journey

My private practice is intensive, so I almost always work with parents who are deeply invested in their children. Otherwise, they would not have agreed to work with me because it requires parental involvement.

Part of my intensive model is that I don't just work with the family. I include everyone who is involved with the child, which means I spend a lot of time in schools working with teachers individually. As you may know, I also work with schools and teachers to bring behavior knowledge to educators, since so few actually get the training that is needed.

Let me be honest, I have met some teachers who might be categorized as "uncaring." It wasn't easy to watch their apathetic attitude toward children in their classrooms. When I scratched beneath the surface, however, the truth that emerged was always more complicated than what appeared at first blush.

Maria's teacher vanished every time I came into her classroom, either into a pile of important papers or into an intense situation with a student, or she actually left the room. As soon as I arrived for each visit, she asked me what time it was going to be over, then quickly found tasks to occupy herself completely. She had a different excuse each time I visited. There were always urgent and more important tasks than the behavior challenges she faced with Maria.

One visit, I made a direct request to her to please stay with me (I actually e-mailed in advance to set it up). I asked her to assist with some of the strategies we were putting into place for Maria. To my surprise, she did. I was so excited! I noticed, however, that during the session there were tears in her eyes each time this five-year-old student did something "weird." This is of course not the technical term, but it is the word the teacher used. She was very concerned about those behaviors—the impact on her friendships and on her learning. Each time Maria would start to act out, this teacher would turn to me and start justifying the behavior.

Did the teacher care, or did she not care? Upon closer examination, I discovered a heartbreaking story.

What This Means for Your Family

Are you one of the parents who stresses about the difference between those habits that are created at home and those created at school? Are you worried that you cannot create the behavior you want without teacher support? It is true that when parents and teachers collaborate, children do better in school and home. There is a lot of research, including my own dissertation, to support this.

Sometimes, for reasons outside of your control, it is not possible for the teacher to be involved, or involved in the ways you envision. When that is the case, remember small beings are smart and can distinguish between what they need to do at home versus at school. Let's keep that in mind in order to create the behavior that is needed for your family to run smoothly!

Your children essentially split their waking hours between time at home and time in school. The structure and support you create at home may be different than what is created at school. Trust that you can create the family of your dreams regardless of the disparities in environment.

When you interact with your child's teachers while your small being is around, make objective observations about how the two are interacting with each other. I looked closely at Maria's teacher's behavior and saw that she needed to escape. That wasn't for lack of caring. Actually, quite the opposite—it was because she cared too much that she could not bear to witness her student's odd (to her) behavior. She was scared and felt like a failure as a teacher when she did not know how to address the behavior. The only way she knew how to cope was to leave the sessions and trust that I was doing my job. With that knowledge, I was able to create a plan to integrate this teacher into Maria's development.

After gaining an understanding of Maria's teacher's motivation, my attitude toward this situation went from frustration to compassion. After every school visit, I told her three great things that happened that day and how I handled one challenge we faced. She was not used to hearing that this student did anything well. I was always realistic, letting her know that some things that were great were below age level while assuring her that this did not change the fact that her student did great.

Maria's teacher started to gain confidence. When I taught her the concrete tools I used in challenging behavior, she was able to ask questions for the first time. A dialogue between us began. This teacher started using my tools, and we made substantial progress. It was clear that she had always cared but couldn't see past her feelings of failure to face the behavior and change it.

As a parent, it is not your responsibility to train your small being's teachers. My hope is that you never come across this situation, as your child's teachers and school should be professionals. However, when there are behavior problems, parents are often called on to address the situation. The reality is that teachers are also human. When you can understand the emotions they may have that impact your child's learning, you have a better chance of taking the steps needed to get on the same page.

Your Small Steps

Instead of blaming teachers for a child's negative behavior, focus on creating a strong set of rules for your family. Once you achieve success with the rules within your family and you have a positive relationship with your children's teachers, you can share those rules with the teachers. Share stories of how the rules worked for your small being and explain to the teachers how to do it themselves. Even if they do not seem interested, they might actually be listening. Be the model of the big being that your small beings need. That will help build a positive relationship with a teacher faster than anything else!

Part 1

Start the process with your family as a foundational learning environment!

Treat your family like an educational experience. Create clear expectations and rules for the behavior that you expect by talking about them each day. I recommend creating your family rules with three succinct behavioral expectations. Write them while thinking about your small beings most challenging behaviors and situations. If she can meet those goals at the hardest times, it is more likely she can meet them in easier times. Every time your small being can meet your standards, that encourages you all to keep achieving excellence.

Make sure to write the rules in positive, action-based language. For example, "Stay in your seat during mealtime," is easier to follow than "No getting up from the table." It tells your child exactly what to do and when to do it. She can then meet those expectations and know for herself if she made it happen or not. This will lead to the success of your small being within your family.

When your children completely understand your expectations, they will meet them. When you are vague in what you expect, your small beings will miss the mark and many times not realize that they did so. Keep your rules clear and phrased in positive language to set your family up to be a successful, well-functioning environment.

Part 2

Stop blaming teachers. Recognize you do not have the entire picture, and accept that your child's school and teacher have reasons for their lack of communication with you. Whether you are in the dark or simply do not agree, throwing blame does not help your child. Focus instead on building a strong, positive relationship with the teacher, one step at a time.

Share your small being's positive moments with your child's teacher. Helpful stories are those that let the teacher know about the amazing person that is your child. This is the first step in building a positive relationship. Simply share the good experiences you have with your child. Even if you don't always feel super positive about your child or see many good moments, there is at least one. Uncover it and share it with the family and your child's teacher. If the teacher knows you are invested in creating a positive educational relationship, he or she will be more open to building a relationship with you. Most parent-teacher relationships are built when problems arise, so letting them know about good news is entirely new for them. It might take you weeks or months of sharing positive stories for the relationship with your child's teacher to solidify.

These positive conversations form the foundation of a relationship that will help you, the teacher, and your child. Your small beings will notice the conversations about their good behavior and it will lead to more positive behavior. As for the teachers, they will feel that you are invested in their classroom, and that is one of the most important elements of building a positive relationship with a teacher. Show the teacher how much you care!

The Smallest Step

Take action in your family by creating clear rules and rewards and consequences for how those rules are followed. Share these rules with your child's teachers so they can see how well your small beings can behave.

NOTES

Scenario 15: His Teachers Are the Behavior Problem

Dr. Marcie's Journey

One of my recent workshop flyers said, "Your kids don't come with a manual." After the presentation, one of the participants, Shelly, introduced herself and wanted to know how we can change that. She had her master's in education and found that while in some elements of teaching she was confident, behavior was not one of them. She desperately wanted a manual for her classroom because she felt so lost about what to do when kids acted out. In our initial conversation, she even mentioned how frustrated she was when parents asked her for guidance because she had nothing to share. She knew she looked like the problem. While I don't ordinarily have teachers (or parents) ask me for a manual, the essence of her question is quite common. People say to me all the time, "I've tried everything and feel clueless—tell me what to do step by step."

Because I didn't have a manual to give Shelly (and it was before I had published my books), I suggested we start working together, especially after she told me about a child, Ali, in her current classroom. With the materials that we gathered through our work—notes and important points from phone-session recordings, notes from my intensive classroom visits, ideas she pulled from my blog postings—she began to make her own behavior manual. It was incredible to watch it come together. She went back regularly to this living document to check for ideas and make sure that she stayed on track.

While you are not working this closely with teachers about behavior, it stands as a lesson that teachers are great advocates when they receive solutions for the behavioral challenges they face. All adults can make a behavioral turnaround just like children can.

What This Means for Your Family

When you have a solid family structure for behavior, even the small being who deals with the most classroom chaos will follow your directions. It's important to have family culture set in place before school and school activities influence your children. Don't wait for teachers to be the only ones who educate your small beings and set up expectations for how to behave in the world. When home and school environments mix, you may see some new behavioral challenges in your small beings. Be prepared.

A child may be an angel at home, but when he goes to school and his friends behave in inappropriate ways, his behavior falls apart, too. The reports you get from school are confusing and sometimes sound like they must have mixed up your kid with someone else's. It's like you have a different child on your hands between home and school. Could this be a case like Dr. Jekyll and Mr. Hyde?

Nope! It's simply a case of a smart child who knows he can play by different rules in different environments with different adults. Happens all the time!

Your Small Steps

Your role is to encourage and expect your child to maintain high standards of behavior you have set at home whenever he is outside of your home. The positive behavior must remain, even when the environment changes. The best way to do this is to be clear with your small beings and the adults who spend time with your small beings. Defining the boundaries between you and a teacher requires clear communication.

Your Rules, Your Family

Just like you have house rules for your small beings, create school rules. Make it clear to his teachers what the behavioral expectations are in your family and for your child. Let teachers and parents of other children in the class know that these rules are constants and are the same for all environments. Decide on how you are comfortable communicating this to teachers and follow through with it. Be willing to step in and step up in front of teachers and/or other parents in his classroom, as needed.

Be the model of how to control behavior. It may be what this teacher is waiting for. What you are doing is avoiding conflict. I know it might not feel that way, as you are essentially telling your child's teachers how to do their job. You are being *pro*active by stating the rules in advance, rather than being *re*active by waiting for a conflict to arise first. The reactive path rarely feels good and often creates a mess. This way, if challenging behavior occurs, everyone will know what to do, and teachers can then work *with* you, rather than possibly have to contradict you.

Make it clear in your expectations that your child's teachers may speak with you about their ideas for alternate approaches after the challenging behavior is handled. Everyone has his or her own strategies and ideas, but you know what works best for your child. As a parent, you need to listen to the teachers, hear their ideas, and respect each of them as a person. Collaborating with your child's school about policies may also be helpful in this moment. Ultimately, the point is to come to an agreement of how challenging behavior will be addressed while your child is in school.

Modeling Behavior

Teachers work hard to understand how to best interact with your child, yet few have any formal training with behavior. It does not make sense to me either, but the education system for training teachers does not include a segment on understanding behavior. You, as a parent, know your child better than anyone else. Use your expertise with your child to provide guidance and to be the role model for the teacher when you can. This means communicating in a clear, calm manner and meaning what you say.

Throughout your interactions with educators, I recommend having compassion. Before I started working with Ali's teacher, she was unwittingly part of the problem. She was not trying to make her students behave badly; she simply did not have the right behavioral tools. There are many teachers who fall under this category and there are success stories that come from their efforts to rectify the situation.

In the case of Ali's teacher, she had been teaching for three years and found that each year the classroom dynamic was very different. She needed to craft behavioral strategies that were unique to each year. This is difficult! Many of the teachers with whom I work have a teaching style that works great for one group of children and not for others. Could it be the same in your family? Your parenting style is great for one of your children and not so great for another. When they do learn more strategies, it takes some trial and error to match them to a particular child. Ali's teacher persisted and she consequentially made substantial changes that led to her entire classroom thriving.

While not all teachers are going to dive in with both feet as fast and deep as this teacher did, remember that as a parent, you know a lot about your small beings and how different tools work for your children. Teachers are meeting your child for the first time in the beginning of the school year and figuring it out as they go. Let's share our tools with teachers rather than blame them.

The Smallest Step

Decide what you would ideally do the next time there is behavioral conflict with your small being in his or her classroom. Consider having a conversation with your child's teacher about how to create that ideal scenario, as problem behavior is bound to happen.

NOTES

Choose Honey, Perspective Is Powerful

PART THREE

All too often, we end up focusing on the things we don't want little ones to do. For instance, you might say within a span of a few minutes, "Don't touch that," "Stop yelling," and "Stop fidgeting so much." Sound familiar? We go through the day speaking to small beings in the negative. It sort of works, but many times at the end of the day, everyone is grumpy, exhausted, and feeling a bit worse for wear. This approach is filled with vinegar.

What would your days be like if instead they were filled with honey-like phrases such as, "Yes," "That was great," and "Thank you"? These can be regular phrases you use throughout the day with your small beings. All you need to do is maintain consistent focus on what you want, rather than what you don't want.

Only when small beings know your expectations can they meet or exceed them. When you're starting a new adventure, talk to small beings about what is to come and exactly what you expect from them. Do you need them to sit quietly for a bit (like when commuting on public transportation)? Do you expect them to only look and keep their hands in their pockets (like at a museum)? Do you expect them to keep their ears and eye open and to be alert to the setting around them (like when playing a game of Eye Spy)? Let them know before beginning each and every adventure, even when it seems redundant. When you repeat your expectations each time you start an event or outing, you are less likely to waste time on corrections.

If your small beings meet your expectations, then give praise and be excited about a job well done! This will require forethought on your part. Otherwise you will spend too much time and energy on corrections if you don't plan this way. Instead, spend time building good behavior to avoid wasting it correcting bad behavior!

If you start an adventure and don't tell children what your expectations are, it is much more likely that they won't meet them. You will end up spending time correcting behavior and talking about what was done wrong. Your frustration will build, and your small beings will feel as if they failed. Please recognize that in either scenario you are expending energy. It may take some work to create this shift, but it is certainly worth that effort! Setting yourself up for a negative result is draining for everyone involved.

It is worth saying that the foundation of these changes is your mind-set. If you dread the weekends and live for school to be in session, then you are encouraging negative behavior in your children, whether you know it or not. You need to be a role model of the positive perspective you want your family to have.

Think about it: You get to spend your time with your kids! Dig deep about all the reasons why you wanted to have children in the first place. Can you feel the fire that brought you to the place of wanting a family? Is it possible for you to slowly begin enjoying your children and ultimately your life overall? How might you make the daily chores engaging for yourself? Is it possible to create adventures that interest you *and* take care of life's daily necessities? If none of these things excite you, then—honestly—dig deeper!

Your mind-set sets the tone for your family. At this point, you may realize that you have a negative view toward parenting and toward your small beings. If you have even a shred of hope within that well of disappointment, then I say start making some changes to make things better. There are small steps you can take toward changing your mentality.

Try some of the following suggestions:

- At the start of every day, tell yourself you will enjoy it. Eventually you will.
- Find ways to talk about your family in a positive light.
- Consider how you can phrase stories about your small beings and start tilting them toward a positive light, rather than a bevy of complaints.
- Stop "war stories" with other parents. This only adds to your negative perspective.
- Create strategies to conquer bad behavior and problems that you experience. You and your small beings deserve better than that.
- Decide you will be the parent who can turn any situation with your small beings into a positive one. This frame of mind will give you confidence.
- Interpret the difficulty of challenging behavior as a mystery waiting to be solved.
- Understand that you are the one in control of behavior in your family, and that when you have a positive attitude, it will infuse itself into your children. Behavior will change simply because you are full of honey!

Action Steps for "Choose Honey: Perspective Is Powerful"

1. Notice the words you use. Are they positive or negative?
2. Observe the small moments when your words are negative. There's no judgment here, just a simple observation.
3. Notice the behavior of the small beings around you in that moment. Is it behavior you want to continue or behavior you would like to change?
4. If it is behavior you want to maintain—great! Keep up those actions. If it is behavior you want to change, then determine what behavior you prefer instead. Get really clear on what the new behavioral interaction looks like and write it down.
5. Keep your paper out, and write down why this behavior change is important. What makes that reaction better than what you are currently experiencing? Find clarity around why this behavioral shift is critical.
6. Begin to take small steps to catch more flies with honey than with vinegar. Take one moment at a time and practice this principle.
7. Celebrate each moment that you use a positive approach rather than a negative one. Notice how the small beings around you act. Celebrate with them when they have the behavior you desire.
8. Keep taking small steps until you are catching your flies with honey the majority of the time. It is an ongoing practice for us all!

Now that you understand how this rule may be applied in general, let's explore some specific situations where "Choose honey: perspective is powerful" may be integrated into your own family.

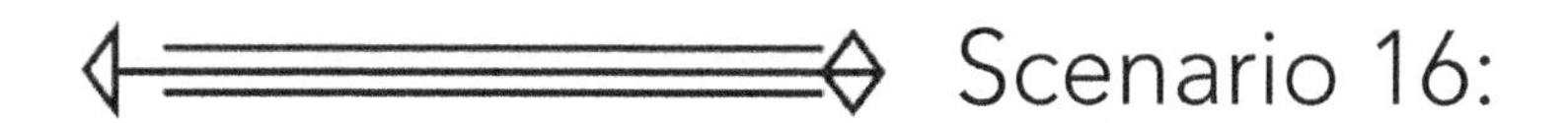

Scenario 16:

I'm So Frustrated

Dr. Marcie's Journey

Small beings rarely frustrate me. Big beings do, especially those who pledge that they really want to change a small being's behavior, but follow that up with a list of excuses as to why the behavior will never change.

When I conduct workshops, there is often one parent with this stance. At one particular workshop, I challenged this parent in her beliefs and discovered the real reasons behind her frustration.

If you have never been, my workshops are rather interactive. We all learn best when we absorb not just with our mind but also with our body, and I aim to give the highest possible learning experience to participants. One parent who sat in the front row answered more questions than anyone and was always the first to raise her hand. She spoke about her small being's aggressive behavior. I gave her one suggestion, and she quickly shot back with a reason why it would not work. I gave a second suggestion, which she immediately let me know she had already tried to no avail. She also shot down my third and fourth suggestions. Her mind-set frustrated me, to say the least.

I took a moment to pause and collect my thoughts. There were a few hundred parents in front of me. I decided to make this a lesson, so I turned to the audience and asked if anyone could see what was happening. A few people nodded yes in reply. I continued, "Is this what is happening to you? One child does something to frustrate you and it takes away from the bigger picture?"

I talked about how I was frustrated and needed to change gears before finishing my answer to her question. I went through my thought process out loud. Was the parent doing this to frustrate me intentionally? No, I concluded. Was she doing it to get attention? Maybe. Was she doing it because it felt good to her? Yes. Was she genuinely interested in this question? Yes. Was it personal? No. My job, I told the audience, was to find a new way to solve this puzzle, get curious, and take a new route.

What This Means for Your Family

First, recognize that you, like most parents, have almost no training in behavior. Most teacher-training curriculums do not include this facet of the successful teacher's toolbox; let alone parent-training curriculums. Without an understanding of the basics of behavior, you will become frustrated. So, if you are having that feeling, give yourself a break. You are reading this book and gaining new acuity with each chapter. By the end of these pages, you will make huge leaps by integrating each of the fundamentals into your parenting practice.

Secondly, it will help enormously to not take any behavior personally. Your frustration will decrease significantly when you learn that the children in your family are not acting out as a personal attack on you. Yes, they are your children, but that does not make the behavior personal. Your child does not hate you, and the child does not mean to make your life difficult. There are no formal statistics on the matter, but I am certain that has never been the case in the history of parenting! Kids do not act out to make you miserable. Instead, think of the behavior as a form of communication (because that is what it is). You simply need to understand the underlying message. Behavior is about conveying a need, so see if you can figure out what that need is.

Your Small Steps

As a parent, you have the most difficult and the most invigorating job ever. Each day, your children's lives are changed because of the time you spend with them. Celebrate that! The good news is that there is a behavioral solution to your frustration! Simply remove the focus from your negative feelings and instead put it into finding behavioral solutions for your children. Doing this requires a degree of acknowledgment about what being a parent actually means. Accept the fact that doing so is not easy.

Getting your children to focus and learn and being amazing humans is a high art. While ultimately solving the problems is hard, finding a way to reduce your frustration is simple. Welcome the fact that each day brings new challenges. Get excited about these challenges, rather than getting aggravated by them. Your role is to teach your children, and dealing with behavioral problems is par for the course. It is your responsibility. You will find the right tools once you decide that you are intent on solving behavioral issues. Stop wasting time on your own hurt feelings and step into your role as a parent and as a leader of your family.

Back to the workshop: When I gave myself a moment to look at the situation, it came to me that she did not truly want an answer. She wanted to feel that she was right and to be validated in thinking that her kid was simply bad and that no one could help. Needing validation for your ideas is natural but also a distraction from thinking clearly about a situation. When I explained that concept, she paused and ceased arguing with me. She knew then that her underlying motivation clouded the path to changing the behavior of her small being. By holding on to the need to feel validated in her abilities as a parent, she was unable to progress; when she let it go, she found the way forward.

On my end, it was necessary that I got on the same page with her and let go of my need to show this woman (and everyone at the workshop) that I was right and that she should just follow my directives. When I took a step back to evaluate the situation, it was apparent that she just needed confirmation that she was a good parent and person, and needing help for her challenging situation did not change that fact.

I work with behavior on a daily basis so, yes, it is easier for me to make those adjustments, but I hope that this story demonstrates that it is possible for you to own your fears and take the next step. No behavioral change is possible if we stay in the role of needing to be "right" or "good." Recognizing this makes it so much easier to take a step back, focus on objective behavior, and make positive behavior changes happen.

Here is a game plan for dramatically reducing your frustration level:

1. Write down the three most frustrating behaviors your small beings engage in each day. The behaviors need to be something that happen at least three times a week. If they do not engage in it that often, that's great. You may want to consider switching behaviors, so you focus on the most disruptive ones first.
2. Write down five different reasons your child might engage in this particular behavior. None of these can include things that have to do with you. A child who never cleans up after herself might do so because of the following reasons:
   (a) She doesn't understand what "clean up" means.
   (b) She has a hard time physically putting items away because her fine motor skills are limited.
   (c) She likes the attention she gets when you personally remind her to clean up.
   (d) She would rather talk with her siblings or keep playing than clean up.
   (e) You only just started to ask her to clean up and mean it.
3. Look over your reasons. Explore the one or two that feel the most accurate. What can you do to help in each situation? Find ways to teach your small being rather than simply being frustrated by her. In the example above, maybe the third option feels right.

Let's find a way to give her that attention for cleaning up, rather than when she doesn't clean up. Right when you ask her to clean up, walk over to her and give her a specific thing to put away. Congratulate her on doing it! Ignore her behavior when she starts roaming around, instead give her another specific thing to put away. Repeat this process, and after a few successful days ask her what she wants to put away. Once she has responded, cease speaking with her until she has completed the task. Congratulations! You subtly shifted the process for how she received attention with honey.

4. Celebrate the small steps that your small being is taking. Talk with her about her progress rather than complain about her behavior. Keep reminding yourself that not one of the behaviors is personally directed to you.
5. Repeat these steps for each behavior you want to change.

The Smallest Step

Every day, recognize one good thing about your small beings and one good thing about your family overall. Remember why you love them, and that will reduce your frustration.

NOTES

Scenario 17:

I'm in Over My Head!

Dr. Marcie's Journey

All parents feel in over their head sometimes. There's no need to get upset about it. Rather you can take it as a sign that you're growing and learning and that you're human. It's an exciting place to be. You're progressing and learning new skills. This feeling reminds me that I need to ask for support and seek out help.

I can remember the first time I felt like I did not have the tools to help a small being. Theresa was seven years old, wasn't on the autism spectrum, didn't have ADHD, or any type of learning disability, but she did show signs of being psychologically unstable. Theresa described in detail to me the people she talked with in her head. These were not imaginary friends, but actual voices in her head from her description. Her family was concerned, and so was I.

I was immediately upfront with her parents that this kind of psychological behavior was not my specialty. I was happy to keep working with them and had several ideas about how to support their daughter, but I did recommend they find someone with more experience in this realm. They wanted to stay with me. This was exciting, but I knew I would need help. Because they wanted to stick with my practice, I reached out to a psychologist with decades of experience dealing with children with psychological challenges. He agreed to provide me with supervision.

The results of this collaboration not only solved the behavior problem for this child, but also taught me about the power of reaching out for help and adequate supervision when necessary.

What This Means for Your Family

Feeling overwhelmed is an emotional experience, not a behavior. It is up to you to figure out how to deal with your feelings before they manifest into behavior. Everyone reacts differently to feeling overwhelmed. Some people will rise to the challenge, take massive action, and make huge behavioral progress. Other people freeze in the face of overwhelming thoughts. What you do is a choice. Let's find ways for you to make progress!

The feeling of being in over your head is one of the telltale signs that you're a good parent. You care enough that you're bothered that you might not be doing a good job. I wish every parent and educator cared as much as you do! Give yourself credit for this quality.

The next step is to reach out for support. This is what I did in the case of Theresa, who appeared to have psychotic symptoms (the family's term, not mine). I reached out for help as soon as I felt like I was in unfamiliar territory with Theresa's challenges. My supervisor and I met every two weeks. I told him how things were going in our sessions, and he provided thought-provoking questions and insights. He used a mix of positive reinforcement and direct feedback to guide me to areas of exploration to apply to future sessions. Today I continue to use the structure he provided in my sessions. I encourage you to seek out similar guidance when you feel like you have reached an impasse with your children. It may look slightly different since we are talking about your family and not your profession, but either way, support is support!

Your Small Steps

Step 1: Understand That it's a Normal Feeling

Admitting that you are overwhelmed and asking for help will make you a better parent! Your small beings will understand that we are all human in our limitations and that we all need help. Own these moments rather than trying to hide them. It is a critical lesson for your children to learn.

The first thing to do when you start to feel overwhelmed is to accept that it is part of the normal cycle of life and raising a family. You have never done this before and as I stated earlier in the book, there is no manual for this. The responsibilities and actions required of you on a daily basis are immense. Every parent, even the ones who seem infallible, have felt overwhelmed at one time or another. Expect to feel this way often and never take it as a sign of failure. The tendency will not go away, but it will lessen over time.

Internally, you may feel incapable of being a good parent and may tell yourself many stories to support this idea, but feeling overwhelmed does not make you a bad parent. It just makes you a parent. Reach out to friends and family and professionals for tips on moving away from this mental block. They will have plenty to share, as everyone has been there!

Step 2: Move into a Better Mental State

Pick a physical activity that you can do for five to ten minutes. This may range from putting on some Tina Turner and busting a move to going for a short run to calling a friend while going for a walk. There are a million ways to celebrate through motion. The goal is to get you out of your head and into your body.

Once you are back home, select one tiny task that you can accomplish in the next fifteen minutes. It could be writing up a grocery list, throwing in a load of laundry, or finally sending in that application for dance classes. You conquer overwhelming feelings by breaking down what you need to do into small, action-based steps, and then taking the first step.

After finishing this one task, do your physical activity again! Then complete two action-based steps and celebrate again. The goal is to continuously enjoy that you are making progress. There is no need to wait until everything is done to celebrate. Think about it: if you have a paying job outside your home, do you get paid just once at the end of the year? That would be way too long to wait for the reward. The same idea applies here. Celebrate after each small step.

Keep in mind that you can celebrate with your small beings. You can also have your small beings help you with the tasks *you* need to get done. Don't get stuck thinking these tasks need to be taken care of *without* your children around. It's easy to get overwhelmed when you look at the big picture and all that you need to ultimately accomplish.

Breaking anything down into small enough steps makes it achievable. It's okay to feel overwhelmed. Take small steps. Small steps will lead to the big changes that will help you feel positive about being a parent again.

With this process, you create a positive association about feeling overwhelmed. Yes, it is a bit Pavlovian, but it will work! Connecting feeling overwhelmed with a physical activity you enjoy and then taking your first step can become the way you face challenges everywhere in your life. Soon you will notice that when you feel overwhelmed you will take these steps naturally!

Keep taking consistent strides. Don't look back and wonder if you did it well enough; just keep moving. If you're a perfectionist, work on that when you're not overwhelmed. In this moment, focus on progress and block out everything inside telling you that you can't do it.

Applying This to Your Small Beings

When your small beings come to you feeling overwhelmed, put together a plan for them using the principles stated above. Keep that program in place for at least two weeks. Part of what makes behavioral change itself feel overwhelming is the expectation that it will happen overnight. It will take time, and that's okay!

The Smallest Step

Acknowledge that you're feeling overwhelmed. It also may help you recognize that it is a feeling. You have control of your feelings and can take actions that keep you moving forward while you are feeling overwhelmed.

NOTES

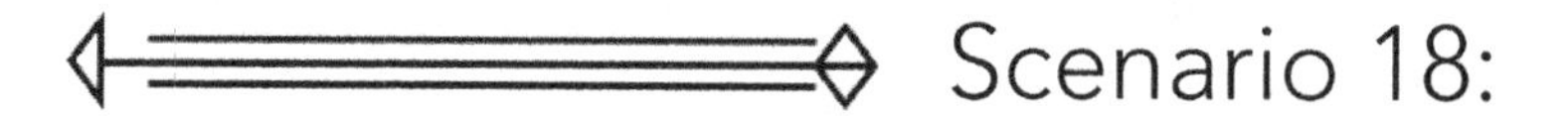

Scenario 18:

She Likes Being in Trouble

Dr. Marcie's Journey

Because I work with children who exhibit very challenging behavior, I hear this story all the time. It is a misconception. Kids may appear to really like being in trouble and will egg the frustrated people on, smiling or laughing when adults reprimand them, but this is not the case.

I received a call from a family whose son (let's call him Jake), was just asked to limit his kindergarten attendance to half days. The school thought it would be better for him because he had a diagnosis of oppositional defiance disorder (ODD). As I started to learn more about the situation, I made a request to do a school observation. During drop-off time, Jake refused to go into the classroom so he could stay with his mom for thirty minutes. He smiled while out there and was rather physical when his teachers tried to take him into the classroom. Everyone offered various conversations, promises, and bribes to Jake to try to get him to simply walk into the classroom.

He finally went into the class and sat at his desk. After fifteen minutes, he started to roam around the room, watching his teachers the entire time. When he refused to sit back down, he was walked to the director's office. She talked with him about the importance of listening to his teachers. He listened nicely, colored a bit while he "calmed down," and then went back to class. Within the hour he was back in the director's office for pushing another child. His father was called to pick him up, and he left school earlier than the half day that he was scheduled for. The small boy looked delighted to go home with his dad.

Although Jake seemed happy, no one else was that day. The underlying message in his behavior was a bit different.

What This Means for Your Family

No one wants to get into trouble. If your small being knew another way to get his needs met, then he would do it. This child had a familiar pattern that worked. The joy children like this find in getting into trouble is not the sign of a demon child, but rather the sign of a child who needs better tools!

To begin digging deeper, ask yourself what he likes about getting into trouble. The challenging behavior provides him with something that he likes: control, escape, or attention. Specifically it could mean one or more of the following:

The attention

The predictability

The control
The capacity to create chaos
The power
The reaction of other classmates
Getting out of something hard or boring

The list could really go on and on. The answer to that question is the key to solving the behavioral mystery. Once you find which of these he is actually going for, you can show him a way to get that need met much more appropriately.

Your Small Steps

Before you begin to craft a strategy, you need to believe that your child can change. When you believe he is capable of behaving in a way that is positive as well as desirable, you will find a way to make it happen.

The goal is to find out what he truly wants and to start providing it in moments of positive or neutral behavior, not just when challenging behavior arises. This will take some out-of-the-box thinking and some new strategies on your part, but you can do it.

Start tracking the behavior (as discussed earlier in Scenario 1) to identify what is happening. Watch the consequences to reveal the pattern. Do this for at least a week, depending on the frequency of the behavior. The less frequently the behavior occurs, the longer you will need to collect data so you have a large enough sample.

Make a plan! It does not have to be a big, long, elaborate behavioral plan. Let's keep this simple so that it is easy for you to implement. If you make it too complex, you will never put it into place. Write it in short hand, hit the highlights, and be exact about the actions you will take when the behavior arises. Make sure to include the positive replacement behaviors you will use instead.

Put this plan into place for at least two weeks, no less. Consistency is a big part of behavioral change! Even when you think it might not be working, keep at it for the two weeks. In order to track your child's progress, maintain the note-keeping method of your choice. Do not rely on your memory. Cognitive science teaches us that our memory is not reliable, so do not don't expect it to accurately convey what is truly happening.

After two weeks, review your plan and the information you collected. See what you need to adjust, make those adjustments, and then keep going for another two weeks. Notice the changes. Celebrate the small successes and be patient. Most importantly, remember that your small being wants to be successful and never truly enjoys getting into trouble. Teach him rather than stigmatize him!

This was how we shifted Jake's behavior. After he left school with his dad because he pushed a classmate, the director said she simply did not understand why he liked being in trouble so much. I said that he does not like being in trouble, but that he *does* like being with her and with his mother and father. Socially, it is hard for him to be in class with so many children and to navigate the multidimensional dynamic. Watching Jake in the classroom, on play dates, and with his siblings, it was clear he felt other children are unpredictable and confusing. He preferred to be with the director, coloring in the office, or at home with grown-ups, playing on his own. Getting into trouble was the method he used to get what he wanted.

The family, the director, and I created a new plan. He was able to go visit the director after twenty minutes of good work in the classroom. He was able to call his dad every hour that he remained in the classroom. At home his parents would check on him every fifteen minutes if he had a playmate over or was playing with his siblings. After Jake became successful at those intervals, we increased the amount of time between the rewards. Slowly, the misbehavior disappeared. He acted out because he wanted attention and was struggling. We made the hard times easier and gave attention only for good behavior. The behavior changed!

The Smallest Step

Believe behavioral change is possible, and start to think outside the box. This kind of child won't respond to typical consequences, so see what creative ideas you might implement.

NOTES

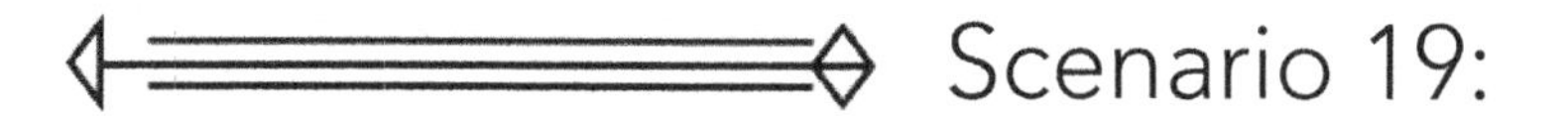

Scenario 19:

My Children Are Ruined by Technology

Dr. Marcie's Journey

I was a child when the original Nintendo came out. My parents gave it to me for my birthday along with the games Super Mario Brothers and Tetris. My sister and I bonded over playing those games for hours.

Our mom, on the other hand, loved spending time with her puzzles. We would spend days doing jigsaw puzzles on the dining-room table. While this pastime did not end, Our mother ended up falling in love with Tetris, too. Do you remember how one turn could last a really long time when a player was good? Our mother was especially good at Tetris; her turns lasted for what seemed like forever.

My sister and I used our mother's love for Tetris to receive permission for more video-game time. We were not allowed to play video games for long stretches, but when my mom participated in Tetris matches, hours would pass without a word from her or our dad. We quickly learned that if we offered her the first turn, she would always say yes to Nintendo time. As a result of our astute manipulation, there were Tetris matches going on constantly in our living room.

Hopefully you maintain more control of technology usage in your home. Small beings will be manipulative to get their fix of technology, so be mindful of that when you are making your family technology rules. There are some positive aspects of video games, for example, in the way my sister and I connected. The goal is not to throw the baby out with the bathwater!

What This Means for Your Family

Technology affects every area of our lives. I encourage you to use it to its full extent within your home and for your family. It can also lead to bad behaviors. It is up to you to be mindful of how technology use is modeled. The subject of technology and small beings could fill another book on its own. It is a large topic and one that many, many people are discussing right now. We will leave that aside in this chapter. The goal here is to gain an understanding of how to address behavioral challenges that may arise in your family around technology.

Your Small Steps

Adults may be just as obsessed with technology as children. The pull of a great TV show, good news on Facebook or Instagram, or a video of a cat playing with a bag is hard to resist. We can become consumed by it.

Model for your small being's enthusiasm without obsession. This means that while in your home with your children you will control your compulsions with technology. Tuck your cell phone away, turn the computers off when you are not using them, and be mindful of the conversations you have about TV shows. If you are using your cell phone for something work-related, be clear and transparent about that. Keeping your personal cell-phone activity just as clear is imperative for you to be able to be present for your children. It may be a challenge, but by halting addictive behaviors around technology, you are giving yourself greater mental clarity and peace of mind. You are also allowing yourself to be present with your family, which is a gift for all of you.

Technology and Children

Dialogue

Have an open dialogue with your small beings. Make the rules about social media, technology, and cell phones clear from day one. Especially if you are first getting them a new device, set the rules up the same day they receive the device. Let friends and family know your rules, too. Your particular family rules will dictate much of the details of what is and is not okay in your home, so make sure you are in line with them. Everyone in your family, including you, will have to follow the family technology rules.

Speak with your family about how technology is a tool for connection, as well as a distraction. It does not at any time substitute for human interaction, so integrate conversations about alternatives for play together.

Demonstrate

Demonstrate the beauty of technology and how it allows us to connect with family and friends from around the world and access incredible amounts of information. If your small beings are fortunate enough to have their own cell phone, iPad, and/or computer, then lead the way in being grateful for the privilege. Be clear that it is a privilege!

Boundaries

Create structure so that your children will not fight over using the devices available in your home. What are the rules for access and what are the rules for sharing? What games are permitted? When may they access their own apps? These are important questions to consider. Know the answer before your small beings find themselves in a struggle.

Give them time to play on technology and set a time limit before the play starts, preferably by using a timer to indicate the end of the play time. When they have had enough time and the timer goes off, do not be harsh with them about switching gears. Instead, suggest other topics. After they have played Minecraft for long enough, maybe you could suggest going outside and playing soccer. Providing substitute conversation and activities is helpful so that you learn to change the experience.

The Smallest Step

Notice all the benefits technology brings into your home! Initiate conversations with your small beings around the amazing possibilities technology has to offer.

NOTES

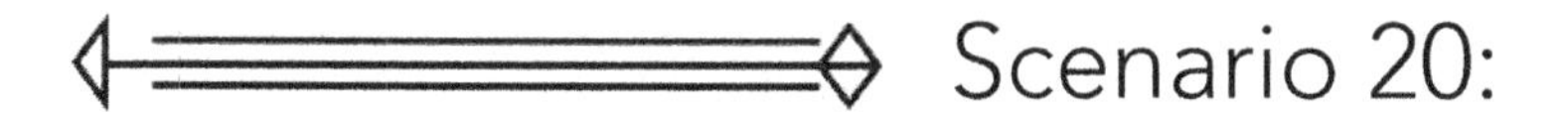

Scenario 20: He Never Makes Eye Contact

Dr. Marcie's Journey

I thought my fifth-grade teacher, Ms. Grima, knew how to do magic. She was sitting in the front of the room, reading *Matilda* to the class. Everyone, including me, was sitting on the rug, listening to the story. I had a dual mission: understand the story and memorize all my friends' birthdays from the chart on the wall. I wanted to be a good friend, and I love birthdays! My teacher called out to everyone, "Eyes forward." She explained that if you are not looking at her, then you are not paying attention. My eyes rested on her before making their way back to the chart. I thought I could do both; no one would notice. My teacher called out, "Marcie, put your eyes forward." How did she know? It was really just my eye line that gave it away, but I thought she must have a superpower!

Eye contact is a major way for you to know if your child is paying attention. Small beings don't always realize that an adult can tell if they are looking or not. They also might not think it is important. You need to make these connections for them.

One of my clients, a five-year-old named Daniel, barely looked at his parents, teachers, but had great eye contact with me and one other therapist. We weren't working any magic; we simply changed the expectation, which I will describe how to do in this chapter.

What This Means for Your Family

We connect with each other through eye contact. We are certain that someone is speaking to us when they look in our direction. A glance can be so telling. No doubt, eye contact is a significant piece of communication.

Eye contact is often seen as a sign of respect, so it may feel disrespectful when your children don't look at you when they talk or when you are speaking. In reality, this may not be the case. Let's not attach a meaning to the behavior that may not be accurate.

Times have changed and small beings are different from what they were when you were growing up. Parents consistently tell me most of the time that their children do not make eye contact. It only took one reminder from Ms. Grima to get me to consistently look at her while she was giving instruction. Your small beings might need a different tactic to get their behavior to change. With consistent small steps, you can do it!

Most likely, your children were never taught that they must look at you when you are speaking, which is great news because it means there's room for you to teach them. Your home will be a much more exciting and satisfying place when everyone is connected and focused, and eye contact will facilitate this. It's definitely worth working on to make this behavior a consistent one among your children.

Your Small Steps

There are two ways I encourage small beings to make eye contact with me:

- Simply wait for eye contact. When a small one is speaking with me, I don't respond or react in any way until he looks at me. Initially, it can take what feels like ages to get eye contact. It is very tempting to give him a verbal or physical prompt, but I have learned over time that if you wait for the eye contact it will become a natural part of communication. For example, I would not answer Daniel's question, give him his snack, or tickle him until he looked at me. That was more powerful than any kind of actionable reminder and it worked every time.
- Don't give them what they want. This is my most effective tool. When a child asks for something, I don't give it to him until he looks at me and asks appropriately. This step is simple and effective! It takes patience in the beginning for each child, but the long-term results are amazing!

As you go through this process, maintain your expectations for eye contact. Too many adults are content when a child asks them a question using kind words, so they stop short of requiring eye contact. Please do not lower your standards! Keep going! You are giving your children invaluable skills for life!

Identify one or two situations you want to improve when eye contact is the most challenged. Most likely, you could do it all day long but that would lead to frustration and burn out all around. To make this a process you stick with, you need to start with just one or two situations. Once you know when and what they are, write the situations down, even if you have a good memory. As a parent, there are so many different things that you keep track of, and writing them down will keep you on task. This process requires focus on your part, and you are setting yourself up for success by limiting your scope.

Make sure to talk directly with your children at least ten times every day in these two situations. Ask them a question and wait for an answer. You will only acknowledge their answers if they meet your eye. Keep repeating the question until they look at you. As soon as they make eye contact, give the acknowledgment and move on to the next point of conversation.

The interaction might go like this:

You: Hi, Daniel. What is the color of the sky?
Daniel: (while looking down) Blue.
You: (wait and keep looking at Daniel)
Daniel: (looking at you) I said "blue."
You: That's exactly right! Thank you.

The pause gives him the time to look at you, and when he does, you provide him with positive reinforcement. After repeating this pattern over and over with different questions, he will start to link looking at you with talking with you. More significantly, he will connect eye contact with your positive acknowledgment, which will increase this behavior in the future.

Once your small beings consistently make eye contact during the situations you selected, move on to another situation. Please be aware that you need to maintain the expectation of that first circumstance. If the behavior starts to slip, you need to redirect them back to making eye contact. Keep the standard high once it has been met.

The Smallest Step

Make sure you are making eye contact when talking with your children. We can't expect small beings to have better behavior than us.

NOTES

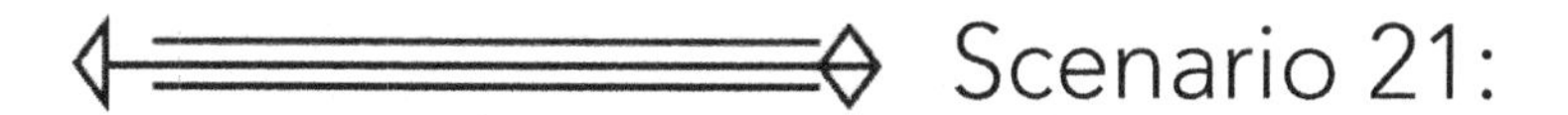

Scenario 21:

She Doesn't Care

Dr. Marcie's Journey

Chloe, a lovely eight-year-old client, appeared to not have a care in the world. Much to her parents' confusion, she did not seem to have a preference for anything. At the beginning of our sessions together, I set up a schedule that included choice time. When it came to those times, she would say it did not matter. Without giving her suggestions, I asked her again to make a choice and waited.

Because of my background in behavior, I understood that beneath Chloe's calm exterior she found it very challenging to make decisions. She was worried she would pick something I did not like. She was fearful that I would judge her for her choices. Our work together was to combat that anxiety, which also happened to improve her executive functioning skills.

What This Means for Your Family

Your child who does not seem to care about anything can break your heart or induce intense anger. She may say that she does not want anything, which prevents you from leveraging positive behavior, or she actively states that she does not care about any consequence you put in place. You can increase the severity of the consequence, like taking away favorite toys or missing play dates, but her seemingly apathetic state prevails.

The truth is that she does care. No small being ever aspires to get into trouble. This is similar to Scenario 12, where we focused on children who should act better but do not. Likewise here: with time you have the ability to reverse this behavior pattern.

First understand that she truly needs help, but does not know how to get it. This is a child who expects to fail. She expects to get into trouble and mess up. When she does, she acts like it was intentional rather than admit to her own failure.

Your Small Steps

You want to use positivity to turn this behavior around. Accept that at this moment, she is doing the best she can do. Praise her for what she *does*, but do not point out everything she messes up. Small beings are human beings, and all human beings want attention. Find a way to give her positive attention and it will shift the dynamic.

If you took the time to notice some good in her, there's a chance that she will find that within herself. Many times, this type of indifference is a way to get attention combined with a lack of certain social skills. She probably has a lot of conversations with adults about her bad behavior. That's a lot of attention. What if rather than repeating the same aggravating and heartbreaking conversation, you provide attention of a positive nature? Point out what she did well that day. She may start to care about something if she knows that you care about her. Yes, this is truly a behavioral approach.

This is the progression I found with my client Chloe, who was the youngest of three children. Her older siblings had lots of opinions and often told her that her ideas were stupid, so my task was to make her feel differently. When she finally came up with an answer, I celebrated it. When she presented ideas, I was always very excited about them. When she voiced her opinions, which meant progress, it was exciting to praise her for this.

Slowly, it became easier for Chloe to say what she wanted to do when she was with me. Her confidence grew. My enthusiasm for her ideas brought out her opinions. She had always had them, but was hiding them. Now she was able to make her voice heard.

Wonder Woman Exercise

The following is a great exercise to do with apathetic small beings. Honestly, I like to do it with all beings☺! It's something you can do with your entire family or with just one of your small beings at a time. Have your child stand up. Ask her to put her hands on her hips and keep her feet wide apart, similar to the classic Wonder Woman pose. Make sure you do it as well. Set a timer for two minutes. Until the timer goes off, together repeat, "I am amazing" over and over and over again. You could dance a little, too!

This is a little silly and a bit crazy-looking, but it does change how you feel. Harvard professor, Dr. Amy Cuddy, has reams of research to support how physical shifts can create psychological and physical changes.

It's hard to get into trouble when you believe you're amazing. When you bolster your small being's confidence through effective exercises and positive reinforcement, you'll notice that your child who seemed not to care, actually does care. She might even confide to you the reasons for her apparent apathy.

The Smallest Step

Know that you are dealing with a child who needs your guidance. Treat her the way you would want to be treated.

NOTES

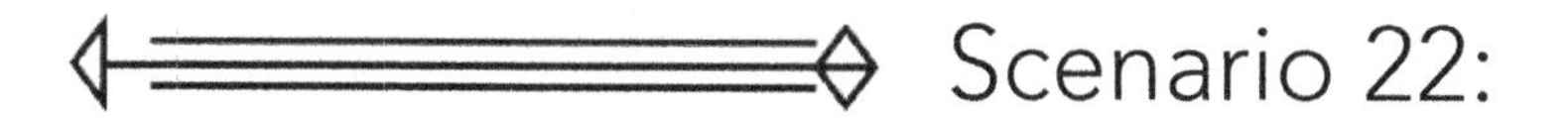

Scenario 22:

He's Doing it on Purpose

Dr. Marcie's Journey

This concept always makes me think about potty training. Kellen was a four-and-a-half-year-old who had potty-training accidents that were quite intentional. To be blunt, this little boy would go into the bathroom, pull down his pants, then pee on the floor. It was hard to deny that he was doing it on purpose.

After he finished, he would find an adult to tell him or her what happened. Because he got some urine on his pants, the available adult needed to clean up his mess and change him. Whoever helped him, be it a parent or teacher, lectured him about his behavior and expressed his or her distress at the situation. I am sure you can understand the person's frustration. Kellen would stand there and watch passively, letting people change him. Punishments were put in place, and all sorts of incentives were tried. Everyone was at his or her wits' end.

From my observations, Kellen was doing this to get

attention. No reinforcement or punishment would impact the behavior. He loved the individualized time with an adult. At home, he was one of three children and had two working parents. In school, there were twenty kids in his class with three teachers. He loved getting someone all to himself!

Based on this understanding, I devised a behavior plan. The adults in his life were to stop talking with Kellen when he had accidents. He had to clean up the floor himself and change his own clothes. Granted, the adult might go back and do a more thorough cleaning once Kellen was done, for hygiene's sake. Paired with that, for every ninety minutes he did not have an accident, he received ten minutes of individual time (measured with a timer) with the adult of his choice. As long as Kellen peed in the potty, he could have the attention he craved. It worked like a charm. Within one month, the accidents stopped completely!

What This Means for Your Family

Behavior, both the kind that big beings like and the kind they do not like, is communication. Whatever you think a small being is doing on purpose is simply this child's way of communicating something important to you.

Small beings love to push big beings' buttons. That sense of control is rather entertaining to them. If a child knows he can frustrate you with a simple action, then you will see that particular behavior more often. Behavior is interactive; if you are having a big response or reaction, then that may be part of why the behavior is sticking around. Small beings find this kind of attention fun.

Remember, it is not personal to you. Like all behavior, it fills a need.

Below are a few universal truths about behavior that are important to remember when dealing with this type of behavioral challenge:

- Consider your behavior as part of the solution to changing your small being's behavior. You can control your response. This is critical.
- Your child needs something that he cannot ask for directly. Try to figure out what that is. Teach the child that he can receive the thing he wants when he acts differently—specifically, when he uses kind language or positive behavior.

Most people behave in particular ways for unconscious reasons. While it might seem that your child is upsetting you on purpose, that is not the case. He is simply trying to fulfill a need the best way he knows how. Have compassion for him.

Your language and actions have a huge impact on how your small being behaves! If you can start believing that your child will do better, then it will show in what you say to your small being and how you say it. This will encourage your small being to shift his behavior.

Your Small Steps

In no particular order, here is a list of ways to remember that your child is not behaving negatively on purpose:

1. If you have more than one small being in your family, select the one you feel is intentionally negative. Write down three behaviors he commonly does that are positive and productive. Also, write three ways in

which you were positive to your child that day. Make a specific time to do this—maybe right after drop off at school or after you tuck him into bed at night. Scheduling the time is critical so that you keep doing it every day.

2. Give each small being in your family three genuine compliments each day. They will know if you make one up! Your goal is to connect to each of your children from a positive standpoint. It also gets your small beings prepared to hear good things about themselves. Vary the reinforcement so your children do not receive the same compliment every day.
3. Create a time in your family when each small being has to say something kind about another family member. This will give you a chance to see new and different wonderful qualities in all your family members. You can provide prompts if needed, but do your best to encourage your children to have their own insights. If one of your small beings has a hard time coming up with something, then it's fine to skip him or her and come back to the child at the end. Never criticize your small being for the compliment he or she gives. You may need to frame a response in a positive light, but do not negate it.
4. Stop complaining about your small beings. Yes, there will be moments when you just have to share a story with someone, but share it once, then move on to the next adventure. Parents often erupt into competitive storytelling for who had the worst moment that day with their child. This only reinforces your frustration and negative view of your children and family. Commit to only telling negative

stories once and never again. Commit to telling positive stories over and over again.

The Smallest Step

Stop asking your small beings "why." It is an impossible question for children to answer when you're angry, and chances are, you already know why.

NOTES

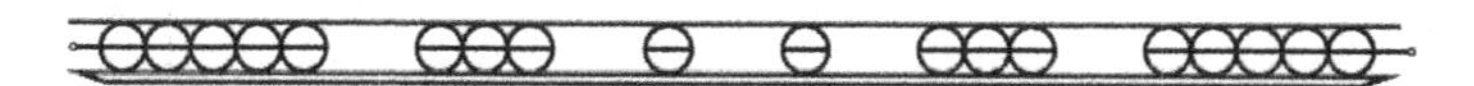

A Powerful Combination

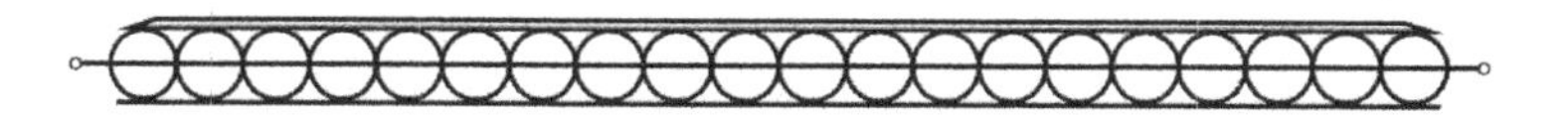

PART FOUR

You've learned about three phrases that are the foundation for behavioral change:

Speak with purpose: words matter.
Do more: actions count.
Choose honey: perspective is powerful.

So far, we have applied each of these separately to individual situations. But some behavioral problems are best addressed by using all three in concurrence. When I face challenging behavior, either within homes, with individual clients, and/or in school settings, I use all of my tools to address it. This comes with practice and consistency. I also use these principles in all areas of my life, including during the writing of both my books.

First, I made sure to speak truthfully about my intentions. Plenty of people told me how difficult it is to write and then publish a book. I responded with, "Interesting, thank you for your thoughts. I am writing a book." If I let my language waver with, "Well, after what you said I don't know, maybe I'll write that book, but I'm not sure now," you probably would not have this in your hands right now.

Then came getting down to writing. My actions were going to get me through this process. When I hit a block, I kept writing. When I became frustrated, I kept writing. When I thought I was done writing, I kept writing. If all I did was say I was writing a book, then this book would not be in your hands.

Perspective was vital. I chose to believe I could complete the task. My belief that parents and teachers could benefit from clear tactics about behavior, and that I had a unique perspective that would help make families, homes, and classrooms outstanding environments was my honey. The positive reasons for working on this project, the honey, always rose to the top when I was overwhelmed or stressed about writing. Focusing on the honey at the end of the tunnel helped me keep going.

The combination of my three keys for unlocking outstanding behavior created this book and my first book. You will find as you move forward with your work that there are plenty of places where you can combine the three keys with your work.

Your Small Steps

1. Notice your behavior. Could you use some more work with any of the three keys?
2. Observe the small moments when problem behavior occurs. No judgments, just observation.
3. Notice your behavior and that of the small beings around you in that moment. Is it behavior you want to continue or behavior you would like to change?
4. If it is behavior you want to maintain, great! Keep up those actions. If it is behavior you want to change, consider what behavior you would prefer. Decide on what you want the children to do in that moment. Get really clear on what the behavioral interaction would look like and write it down.
5. Keep your paper out, and write down why this behavior is important. What makes that reaction better than what you are currently experiencing?

Find clarity around why this behavioral shift is critical.

6. Begin to take small steps to apply any of the tools discussed throughout this book. Take one moment at a time and practice each principle.
7. Celebrate each moment you succeed. Notice the behavioral response for the small beings around you. Celebrate with them when they have the behavior you desire.
8. Keep taking small steps. It's an ongoing practice for us all!

Have you noticed that these action steps are very similar for each part of the book? This is because behavior patterns can always be changed in the same way. You can use the same technique with several different behaviors. It is the repetition of the pattern that helps you continue to grow.

Now that you understand how these rules may be applied in general, let's explore some specific situations where you may apply them as effective tools for your family.

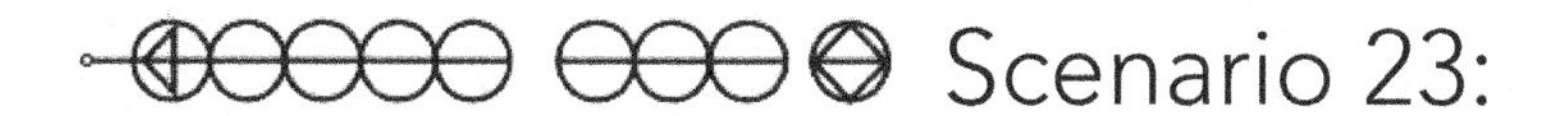

Scenario 23: It Is Impossible for Her to Wait

Dr. Marcie's Journey

I tend not to have favorite kids, but every once in a while, there's one who sneaks deep into my heart. Amya was one of those small beings. She was three years old and showed no capacity for waiting. For example, when she asked for a glass of water, even if I answered right away with "sure" and started to get up to get her the water, she would ask again. She asked the question every two seconds until I handed her a glass of water. Every time the request came, I wondered how fast she thought someone could get her water.

I tried a bunch of different strategies. I tried not doing anything at all, freezing for several seconds each time she asked a repeated question, answering every time she asked with a true answer, and answering with nonsense. I even tried starting over each time she asked again, going back to my chair to get up and get her a glass of water. None of it worked.

It came to me that I had never asked her to wait. The next time she asked for water, I said, "Okay, please wait while I get it." She responded by continually telling me that she was waiting. She pointed out that her body was calm and she was still in the chair. This was true, but why the repetitive communication?

What This Means for Your Family

You might have a small being who is the first to put her shoes on, but then is never ready when it is actually time to leave the house. Or maybe she has a tendency to ask you a million questions when it is time to wait quietly. Both have the potential to drive you crazy.

On one hand, you have to empathize with her, as waiting is hard! When was the last time you just waited? This does not include sending a text, scanning Facebook, reading a book, scrolling through a website, or playing a game on your phone. My guess is that it has been a while! Adults have so many things happening that true waiting does not happen anymore.

The first step in facing your impatient small being is to adjust your expectations. Small beings do not have a model of what it looks like to wait. Most likely, when your small being is asked to wait you give her something to do, like a video game, toy, or cell phone. You are going to have to teach her how to wait. Recognize that you are teaching a new skill, just like addition or tying shoes.

Your Small Steps

Let's create the plan for waiting!

First, you should assess if a simple tweak or two can teach all your small beings to wait:

- Consider if she really needs to wait. Make sure your request is age- and situation-appropriate.
- Think about where your small beings are waiting. Is there temptation around them, specifically toys or electronics they like to play with? Moving to a more spacious waiting location may improve behavior.
- Notice next to whom your child is waiting near when there are behavioral challenges. Waiting near siblings may make it harder or easier depending on the dynamic. Consider having specific waiting spots with you in the middle, if they egg each other on.
- Have you clearly defined the behavior of waiting? What does appropriate waiting look like in clear, objective, and positive terms? Maybe you request that all voices are "off" and hands are placed by their side. Maybe you ask for feet on the floor. Maybe you would like them to stand tall or direct their eyes to you. When you need your children to wait you could say, "Please wait. Waiting looks like standing tall with hands in your pockets and your mouth closed." There is no room for confusion this way.
- Remind the entire family of your expectations every single time they need to wait. This will set everyone up for success. A sentence like, "While we wait our voices are off, our eyes forward, our hands are in our pockets, and our feet are still," will go a long way to remind your small beings

how to behave. Keep in mind that you have to abide by the directions as well.

Most importantly, write down your responses and ideas to the above elements, especially what waiting looks like. I know you already have so many lists and papers floating around, but using the same language with your children day after day will allow them to master this skill more rapidly. Consistency is critical!

When you are clear on what waiting looks like, your small being who is learning to wait will have significant improvements in behavior. If she does not, then here are additional strategies to use:

1. Notice the times when your child *is* waiting and gets excited about them. They may be rare, but I am confident they exist. Acknowledge that she can do it and celebrate that with her. Say something like, "You are doing a great job keeping your hands in your pockets while waiting for dinner." She is more likely to repeat the behavior next time.
2. Set her up for success by giving her attention before she acts out. When you ask your family to wait while you get dinner ready, walk over to her and say, "I can't wait to see how amazing you are going to be while I put out dinner!" Go back to getting food ready. About a minute later, walk by her and say, "Wow! I like how nicely you have your body sitting still at the table!" Maybe even bring her a starter snack as a reward for waiting so nicely. Then as you are putting the finishing touches on the dinner table, use her name and provide a compliment for how great she is doing, like "Amya is sitting so quietly at the table, and is clearly ready for dinner." Here you

are providing attention up front before she acts out. Yes, it takes focus, but you already give her a lot of attention when you do behavior corrections. Now you are in control of when and how you are directing your attention. After two weeks, start to slowly reduce the amount of interactions. Move from three shout-outs to two, then gradually fade down to one.

3. She may need a job while waiting. When you let the family know it is time to prepare dinner, say, "Amya, please put plates out for everyone in the family on the table and let me know when you are done." This gives her something to do while waiting. Please be clear that it is not her job to get other family members ready for dinner, just to put out the plates. Once the job is complete, give her another job, like adding forks next to each plate. When she is focused on her job, it is less likely that she will be tempted by bad behavior. You can also give her a job like counting the number of cabinets in the kitchen or listing all the states in her head. Get creative!
4. Pick one other situation when waiting is hard for your small being and decide that you will not make her wait. Maybe you will make her the last person to get ready, or send her on an errand for you while the rest of the family waits for a show to start. This will reduce any challenging behavior that comes when she has to wait. It will also minimize your need to correct her.

I went through the process described above with Amya. When all strategies failed, I realized that she needed something to keep her voice occupied while she waited. I asked her to count instead of repeating herself. She loved this, as it became a game to see what number she would get to before she got her water. When people were around, like in her classroom, she had to count in her head. Teaching mental math is never a bad thing. Sometimes she counted by twos or fives and other times she counted in Spanish. The variety kept it interesting, and she learned to wait in an active, engaged, and appropriate way.

The Smallest Step

Write out the steps to waiting and share them with your small beings. At least they will have an idea of exactly what you mean when you ask them to wait.

NOTES

Scenario 24: They Are *All So* Rude

Dr. Marcie's Journey

Playing with my friends' children is so much fun. It is a moment when I can take my "Dr. Marcie" hat off and just play. There are, however, certain behavioral standards I maintain, polite language being one of them. It always tickles me when my friends' kids have better behavior when I'm around. Their parents think I'm casting a spell over them, but I swear it's simply being consistent with the rules of behavior.

All of the children in my life—whether they're a client or a friend's child—look me in the eye and respond the first time I call their name. I simply do not tolerate a lack of either of these behaviors and leave no other option than for them to look me in the eye and answer the first time I speak to them.

I also find that a snarky attitude and not saying "please" and "thank you" are unacceptable. All this may make me seem like I'm uptight, but I can assure you I'm a bundle of laughter. I simply have high behavioral standards and the behavioral knowledge necessary to maintain them with small and big beings alike. It's hard enough to get one small being to be polite sometimes; creating a family or classroom full of conscientious children seems impossible. Shifting your family environment will take some work on your end, but you can do it!

With each small step you take, you are closer to creating etiquette in small beings. I saw this happen during a friendly game of Uno one night. One of my friends has three children, and we all spend time together. We were playing Uno, one of my favorite games. Her youngest, Walker, was just learning the rules and thought it was super funny to skip people. When he got a skip card, he put it down while laughing at the person who was skipped. While his own amusement was adorable, I knew that this was a bad habit in the making. I used my adult privileges to make up a new rule. Each time he skipped someone and laughed he got skipped on his next turn. Each time he skipped someone and was kind about it he got the skip card back and could use it again in his next turn. I intentionally did not define kind behavior and wanted to see what he would do. Using the techniques below you will understand how to create the amazing behavior change that I witnessed.

What This Means for Your Family

Twenty years ago, small beings would never dream of doing and saying the rude things that they do now. Uncovering the reasons for this shift would take up another book. It could be the sassy attitude of most cartoon characters or the prevalence of aggressive and apathetic story lines that negatively influence small beings. The root cause could also stem from the fact that parenting standards have changed. All of these things are outside of your control. It's more productive to accept it as it is, including that it drives you crazy, and move on to solving the issues.

Your Small Steps

Small Beings Model Your Behavior

Start by examining your own behavior. Take a good look in the proverbial mirror and spend the next two days objectively observing yourself. Sometimes, what we think we do and what we *actually* do are not the same.

Here are some things to pay attention to: While with your family and around your children, are you gracious and kind? Do you gossip about friends or complain about the world? Do you sometimes sarcastically answer your small beings?

If you notice these and/or other negative behaviors, *stop them now!* Do whatever you need to do. You cannot improve politeness within your children without first improving it within yourself. I repeat that if you are rude, even in subtle ways, the small beings around you will pick that up and undoubtedly model it back to you. Worse yet, if you try to tell them to be polite, your insistence will backfire and spunky children will tell you that you are a hypocrite. So, stop it, stop it, stop it.

You will also want to objectively observe the behavior of other adults who consistently spend time with your small beings. If you notice that they are not exactly models of kindness, then you need to have a compassionate conversation with them. Do not point out their downfalls; simply let them know that you want to focus on reducing your small beings' rude behavior and you realize that all adults need to be that model. If they are resistant, then pull out this book, and show them this chapter. Dr. Marcie is officially telling them to lighten up their attitude. Either do this or humbly agree to never complain about rude behavior in your small beings again.

Once you have your allies to create a polite environment, you're ready for the next step!

Enforcing Polite Behavior

Create an educational unit around polite behavior. Even though you are a parent, not a teacher, you teach your children things every day. This formal teaching will serve you well. Let go of the idea that they should know this already, because they do not. Teach it intentionally. Start a conversation about being polite. What does it mean and what does it not mean? Use multiple examples and different mediums, like videos of rudeness and politeness. Role-play different types of situations that you think will be relevant. Depending on the age of your children, have them draw pictures or write stories to share their ideas.

Once you've spent two to three weeks talking about politeness and you've all shared examples of kind words, you're ready to make this a family rule (or at least an expectation). Communicate this with your small beings. Let them know your expectations and the consequences for polite and for rude behavior.

Positive and Negative Consequences

Polite behavior needs to be rewarded, either with a formal reinforcement schedule—that is, create a new schedule or use part of one that already exists—or through social reinforcement. Make sure to have this in place before you start enforcing the new rules.

Ignore rude behavior to the best of your ability. My favorite way to ignore rude behavior is with confusion. When one of your small beings slips up, and he will from time to time, look at him with a confused expression as if he is speaking another language. Give him some time to come around on his own. Try to avoid giving him a prompt as you do not want him to start to rely on it. Celebrate with him if he corrected himself. Behavior change is underway!

Know that this process will take time. Be patient with yourself and your children as you change this behavior. Avoid all temptation to shame *any* child for being super rude. Put your plan in place, stick to it, make adjustments strategically as needed, and stay focused.

You will notice the pattern of behavior change like in what happened at the end of my Uno game with Walker and his family. After I made the new rules clear, we continued to play, and within a few more minutes, Walker used two more skips and lost two turns. The third time he played, he lay a card down and said, "It's my only blue card. I have to skip you." As promised, I gave the skip card right back to him! He was shocked. The next time blue was the color, he used the skip card again, "It's blue, and I have this skip. You can play next time." Again, I gave him the card back. He continued this way throughout the game.

As the game progressed, Walker's apologies and offers to share his skips became more entertaining. By shifting the dynamic, we taught him to be charming with kindness and not rudeness. You can make these small changes in your small beings and slowly begin to create a more compassionate family culture.

The Smallest Step

Check your own behavior. Speak to your small beings the way you want to be spoken to—kindly and with compassion.

NOTES

Scenario 25: Can I Really Change Her Behavior?

Dr. Marcie's Journey

Before I share my story, I need to answer the question. *Yes*, you can change any challenging behavior. Over and over again, I have worked with families to change behavior that seemed pervasive and permanent and hopeless. Know that whatever problem behavior is happening, it can change! Behavior can always change.

I received a call from a family who had tried everything, or so they said. Their small being, Rebecca, was ten years old. She had attended three schools in the past four years and was seen by five different therapists in that time. Nothing seemed to change her oppositional, defiant, and aggressive behavior. She was diagnosed with a language-processing disorder, so the parents often answered questions for her and anticipated her needs. They walked on egg shells around her, as did her school.

Surprisingly, her school was not interested in support. The family wondered if they alone could impact the problem behavior. Without hesitation I said yes, and we dove in.

The first step was for the parents to start Speaking with Purpose. Then we combined that with Doing More, as in following up their words with actions. Finally, they started using more honey in their daily lives at home. We quickly and intensely worked together to put the three keys in place because the parents became more and more motivated as they saw success.

What This Means for Your Family

You're a parent and you have the capacity to reach your child. Find the best way to support the challenging behavior and know that it can change. This does not make your job easier, but it is part of your job. There is always a way to find a solution to a behavioral challenge—doing so will make you an outstanding parent and increase the joy in your family.

Explore the bigger picture of what your small being needs to thrive. Ask yourself what conversations, evaluations, support, and/or effective transitions need to come together to improve her behavior. Take the right steps to make sure your small being is properly supported. There are limits to what you are capable of, which is why support staff and consulting with experts is critical. Utilize whatever resources you have, both inside and outside your immediate community.

Through all of this special effort, accept that your child is capable of incredible behavior. Stop complaining and focus on what you can do to change her life, the lives of your other family members, and yourself. There is a lesson in every challenge we face.

Do you remember what it felt like to be a child? Whether you loved or hated your upbringing, there was still something inspiring in everyone's childhood. There were adults who inspired you…maybe it was a parent or a teacher or neighbor. Remember that person now and how he or she made you feel. That is how your child views you. You are extraordinary in his or her eyes, and you can help facilitate a turning point in life, right now!

Take that truth and congratulate yourself on the great work that you are doing. You are literally shaping the future. While it may be hard and challenging, you must acknowledge that your work matters to the world. Your small beings might not remember every moment or every conversation, yet they strive to make each one memorable. Make being in your family an incredible experience for all involved!

Your Small Steps

To get you the right help for this situation, I broke down what you need to do by each of my three foundational phrases for behavior change:

Speak With Purpose, Words Matter

Try very hard to mean what you say with your small being. Get clear about your expectations and state them clearly. Each child in your family may need a different set of rules; fair does not mean equal. Stop focusing on behaviors that you are not able to change. Repeating corrections will only frustrate you more.

You are a parent, so act like one. Your child is reachable and needs adults who believe in him or her. If not you, who? Be the parent who inspires your family and highlights the strengths in each family member.

Do More, Actions Count

Take very small steps to show your seemingly unreachable child how to accomplish any goal. Do not over-verbalize to your small being, as it could add to behavioral challenges. Show her what you mean through your actions. This will work for listening skills, like cleaning up when asked, just as much as it will work for social skills.

Choose Honey, Perspective Is Powerful

Be kind to your small beings. Rather than blaming her for being disruptive in your family, find ways to reinforce that she *is* part of your family. You will be the model for your children by showing that you accept the differences in each of your children and love them all.

The combination of these three elements will go further than you might imagine! Within three months, the parents had a small being who followed their directions, helped set the table, and shared toys with his younger sister. It was a remarkable turnaround. The parents began to show the teachers the exact tools to use for their son's success, because he was still struggling in school. Differentiating people and places is something every small being does, so you can use this to create any change you dream of.

The Smallest Step

Be kind to every human, including yourself. Remember, all behavior can change.

NOTES

Making Lasting Change

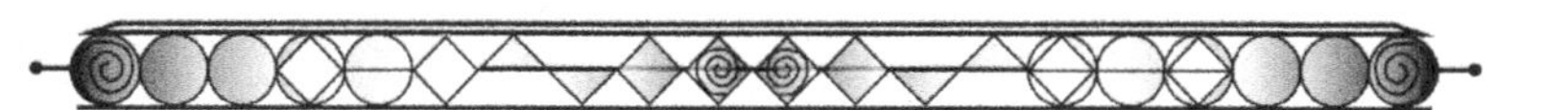

PART FIVE

When it comes to behavior, there are some elements that are critical to highlight—concepts and details to understanding behavior that will help you create lasting change. I created this final chapter to highlight those elements that will keep you on the right track over time.

My three keys to unlock outstanding behavior are a solid foundation for any behavior change:

Speak with purpose: words matter.

Do more: actions count.

Choose honey: perspective is powerful.

Once you master them, your family and your parenting will transform forever. You will love your family again!
Be patient with yourself and take it one step at a time. Small steps lead to big behavior change.

Scenario 26:

Critical Behavior Details

Here are a handful of behavior concepts that will help you as you embark on your journey to change behavior.

Functions of Behavior

Often, we focus on the form of behavior—what the behavior looks like. Did the small being hit or yell or get out of his chair? We talk only about the actions. While the form provides some useful information, it is the function that drives behavior. Function must be uncovered to change behavior effectively.

The fact that there are only four functions for all human behavior always leaves me feeling awed. All of the different emotions, nuances, and forms fit into four functions: attention, escape, self-stimulation (it feels good), and medical.

Attention

Attention-seeking behaviors function to draw much-desired attention to the person performing them. If you have a small being who does many behaviors that result in you talking with him or him having individual conversations with adults, these are most likely attention-seeking behaviors. The way you address these types of behaviors is finding a way to give your small being attention for appropriate and positive behavior. Specifically, provide attention when children have good behavior, and do not provide attention for challenging behaviors.

Controlling behaviors also fall under attention as a function. In order to be in control of another's behavior, that person needs to be providing attention. Picture your child who is always asking you to sit in a specific spot. This small being only has control over you if you listen to his requests and sit in the chair he designates for you.

Escape

Escape as a function of behavior is used when your small being wants to get out of something. If the challenging behavior is followed by your child not needing to complete a chore or direction or task in your home, then the function is escape. When this is the case, the adjustment to make is to find a way to have your child complete the task or direction before a break is received. This can require thinking outside the box for some challenging behavior, but do your best. You want to ensure that challenging behavior is not how your child learns to escape situations. Rather, teach ways to appropriately receive breaks when needed.

When your child engages in escape-seeking behavior, you may want to consider ways that you can increase her ability to sustain a task. It will need to be paired, at least initially, with providing breaks in order to decrease the behavior. However, over time, teaching increased tolerance for bigger chores or situations will support a positive change for your small being's behavior.

Self-Stimulatory

Self-stimulatory behaviors are behaviors that are performed simply because they feel good. We all have behaviors that we engage in because they feel good. They become a problem when they are not socially acceptable. For example, nose picking. Most adults have learned that when there is something uncomfortable in their nose, a tissue needs to be located to change that feeling. The behavior of using a tissue helps us feel physically better while staying within social expectations. Small beings want that same, improved feeling of a cleared nose but may not have learned the social expectations. So, they pick their nose with their finger. It feels good!

The goal with behaviors that are done because they feel good is to teach your small being to find the same or similar feeling in a socially acceptable manner—the equivalent of having the child use a tissue rather than her finger to remove boogers from her nose.

Medical

When behaviors stem from a medical cause, there is little behaviorally that can be done to affect change. The medical community needs to address these challenges. For example, picture your child acting out when you ask him to read the numbers on the clock. You ask him to answer by just saying the numbers, and you know he can do it, but he refuses to give you an answer. It turns out that he needs glasses and cannot read the clock from so far away. Getting him glasses is the only way to change this challenging behavior. No behavior intervention could change his vision. If there may be a medical reason for any behavior you are experiencing, have this function explored first. If you believe your child cannot see something, get his vision tested. Medical functions for behavior should be ruled out as soon as possible.

All Behavior Is Communication

Behavior always communicates a need. Challenging behavior is simply communication. When faced with challenging behavior, remind yourself that your small being is communicating. She is stating a need that she does not have another way to express in that moment. She is stating a need in a way that has worked previously.

Your small being may have frequently interrupted your reading by irritating her sibling. Each time she does it, you stop reading and remind her to stop. Behaviorally, she is asking for attention each time she nudges her sibling, and you have consistently provided that attention. Recognize that this is what she is communicating. Find a way to fill that need for attention when she is behaving well.

Replacement Behaviors

Providing replacement behaviors is a critical element of changing any behavior. A replacement behavior is another way to get the same need met. Teach a positive and socially acceptable way for your small beings to get their needs met.

Think about it: Behavior is communicating a need about wanting attention, needing to get away, or a positive sensation. If you do not teach a replacement behavior, what will happen? Do you think your child will go without having that need met? Nope! Your small being will come up with the replacement behavior. In my experience, the replacement behavior that the child picks is always less desirable than the original challenging behavior.

Part of the overall goal can be to reduce the amount of attention your small being needs. However, in the immediate future, if your small one is getting attention with challenging behavior, you need to teach a way to get such attention with desired behavior. Without this element, a new challenging behavior will arise. Simply moving from one unwanted behavior to another is not productive. So, make sure to include replacement behaviors in your behavior plans.

Extinction Bursts

This is the technical term for when a negative behavior comes back in a burst. It is common and will most likely happen when you start to change behavior. Expect it! When you see this brief increase in the challenging behavior you have been working so hard to decrease, do not get discouraged. Keep going with your strategies. If you keep moving forward, the burst will end and you will be back on track.

Here is the problem: if during the extinction burst you give up, then you lose all the forward momentum. This is the challenge that most adults face. If you don't know about this occurrence, when you see the increase, you think you are on the wrong track. This is simply not true. You need to work through this intense burst. When you do, your hard work is paid off by a decrease in challenging behavior!

Longevity of Behavior History

The longer a behavior exists, the longer it takes to reduce or remove it. Conversely, the newer a behavior, the quicker it is to reduce or remove. This small fact is critical because it allows you to have realistic expectations for a time line of behavioral change. If you have a child who for the past four years never sat in his chair for any meal, you can expect it to take months to teach him to sit in his chair. Having that expectation clear gives you the motivation to stay on track. Similarly, if you have a child who has suddenly begun to get out of his chair at dinner time for the past week, you can start an intervention and expect it to take just a few days to reduce this challenging behavior.

Use this information wisely. When your small beings start to show challenging behaviors, don't wait too long to put the tools in this book to work. Don't wait and hope that he gets it together or stops doing it on his own. Be proactive and provide the support to ensure that the behavior is short-lived behavior!

NOTES

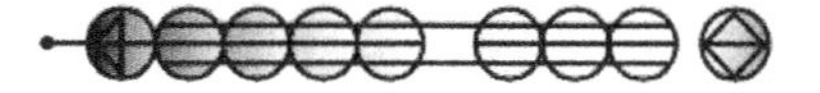

Scenario 27:

Remember What it Means to Be a Parent

You are a parent! Every day you are shaping your small beings and participating in the creation of their future. This is such a privilege! It is also a big responsibility.

Now that you have a better understanding of how behavior works and of specific tools for certain behaviors, it is up to you to put the tools to work. Otherwise, this is just a book you read once. My dream is that you take this knowledge and apply it. This is the beginning of the hard work and you are ready for it!

Let's end by reviewing some great ways to keep you motivated and on track when the going gets rough!

Remember Why You Became a Parent

When I do workshops for parents, I always ask this question: Why did you decide to become a parent? Often, it is a reason that has long been forgotten in the grind of the day to day. Having this conversation lights a new fire! So, get out your notebook and write down why you became a parent and what dreams you dreamed when you thought about growing your family. Keep this in a place you can easily review it when you need to.

As for me, I started this journey because I wanted to help small beings have a brighter future. I believe that if we can help small ones thrive when they are young, they will have a better life. Also, I wanted to spend my days playing. I get to do something that touches my heart on a deep level while playing Monopoly every week? I'm in! That is why I do what I do.

I have the reason I am a behavior specialist in my cell phone under the "notes" section. After a hard session, I go back and read it. It keeps me motivated to complete session after session with all of my focus and attention. I probably read it every two weeks. Yes, I still need the regular reminder of what my work is all about. I bet you do, too.

Share Your Success Stories

Find someone in your life to be your cheerleader. If you can, find more than one. When you face challenging behavior, it can feel isolating and as if no one understands. Find a person who will listen to you as you go through the journey of changing behavior. This is not someone to whom you can simply complain. Choose someone who will make sure you stay proactive and find the productive small steps that are needed to change behavior. This person needs to celebrate your small steps and remind you of the progress you have made.

Staying on track to change behavior takes dedication and motivation. Having support around you will ensure that you stay the course.

Remember You Are an Adult

There are days when we don't want to be the adult; we all have those days. Truth is, when it comes to small beings, we have to find a way to remain the adult. When a small being is pushing your buttons, how can you be a model of appropriate behavior? It is expected that you will be frustrated or upset at times. You don't need to hide those emotions. You do, however, need to respond as an adult. This means no yelling or pouting or holding grudges with your small beings. It means expressing your feelings with your words and moving on when incidents end.

Ultimately, we cannot ask our small beings to behave better than we do ourselves.

Write It Down

Throughout this book, I have suggested you write down different things—from why you want to change a behavior to specific goals to frequency of certain behaviors. Writing helps change behavior in two ways. First, it ensures you are clear. It helps clarify exactly what you desire to focus on and how you will work it out. Holes in your logic, missing elements of your ideas, and misconceptions are more easily seen when you write something down as opposed to keeping it all in your head. Second, it gives you a place to reference as behavioral changes occur. When a challenging behavior like hitting occurs five times a day in your home, it's hard to realize that you have made significant progress because it used to happen ten times a day. Our memories are fallible and unreliable. It's amazing to go back to the beginning of a behavior log and read how bad it was. Reflection is incredibly powerful when it comes to keeping you motivated and on track.

When you share experiences with other adults, teachers, friends, and/or family members, it helps to have written notes. Others will benefit from the clarity of your details and exact knowledge when sharing thoughts about your small beings. Teachers will be able to replicate your changes if you can explain what you did. Notes help! Behavior change sometimes feels like magic if we don't record what we did to make the change happen.

Make It a Daily Habit

Building a family you love takes focus and intentional, consistent action. Teaching small beings to have outstanding behavior requires ongoing attention. The best way to ensure you stay on track is to make monitoring behavior a daily habit.

Many only focus on behavior when there is a problem. When there are the first signs of problems to come, all too often we just cross our fingers and hope it gets better. Don't do that. Don't wait to be reactive. Use these tools in your family every day. The best time to make sure you are speaking with purpose, doing more, and choosing honey is when things are going smoothly! This will ensure that behavior stays outstanding in your family. It will also provide a framework for you to be ready when challenging behavior does occur.

Small steps every day make all the difference.

Remember, blue skies are ahead. We can get there together!

NOTES

NOTES

NOTES

NOTES

Beyond the Book...

Do you want to take these tools and strategies beyond the book? Are you ready to take action and want support to make the tools come to life?

Sign up for Dr. Marcie's
***Love Your Family Again* Course!**

This course dives into the best tools from the book directly from Dr. Marcie.
The videos help bring the tools to life and her additional comments make it even easier to take action steps.

This 6-module program is designed for parents like you—ready to walk into action now.

Sign up today! Go to:
LoveYourFamilyAgain.com

Beyond the Book...

Are you looking for additional ways
to learn about behavior?
Want to take your understanding
beyond the pages of
Love Your Family Again?

Dr. Marcie offers a variety of trainings just for you!
From Boot Camps to Behavior Boosts
From Live in-person to Online Anytime.

Keep learning with Dr. Marcie!

Go to **DrMarcie.com** to find the perfect training for you!

Beyond the Book...

Do you Need Individualized Support?
You read each scenario...
You applied the tools...
You did the *Love Your Family Again* Course...

Yet, you still have questions?
You have behaviors that were not addressed?
You need more support?

While this is not for everyone, there are select families who need customized support and individualized solutions.

Dr. Marcie does individualized consulting.
Email: **Info@BehaviorAndBeyond.net**
Ask Dr. Marcie Anything.

Love Your Classroom Again

Dr. Marcie's first book

The perfect way to share these insights with your Teachers!

Love Your Classroom Again is for educators of all levels who want to rediscover their passion for teaching, love of their students, and excitement to spend each day in the classroom, but aren't sure how.

Get a clear understanding of behavior in a way you've never heard before

Find easy-to-implement tools to deal with the most challenging student behaviors you face

Share strategies used successfully in a wide range of educational settings

Discover a fresh experience of teaching with you fully in charge

LoveYourClassroomAgain.com

Made in the USA
Monee, IL
30 July 2021